CONTRASTING HUMILITY AND PRIDE

RENE LAFAUT, MSc.

Hard-Cover: ISBN: 9798493445767
Paper-Cover: ISBN: 9798583634699

DEDICATION

I dedicate this book to Marilyn Leonard for teaching me the importance of tolerance and for those who have been my teachers in so many areas where spiritual rubber meets the road to reality.

ENDORSEMENT

Rene's writing is very wise teaching that is based on the Gospels and his experience of the Christian life. He has so obviously overcome enormous hurdles. The text is well-edited although
lengthy. But in combination with his on the ground teaching I am sure that this can be very helpful to those who he involves in teaching. He also has good theological instincts.

Bill Reimer, Regent College, Vancouver, BC

CONTENTS

ACKNOWLEDGMENTS

I acknowledge Marilyn Leonard who in many ways challenged me and gave me enough of a push so that this book had a chance of being written

FOREWORD

Rene's down to earth straight-forward defining of component parts of humility and pride, while consistently using our capacity to love as the yardstick of our progress keeps us from sinking in a bog of theology, and sets us in the footsteps of Jesus.

Rene has made every mistake in the book when it comes to pride but the amazing thing is that he has learned from each one of them and brings understanding and a depth of perception to each facet that leads us unerringly back to Jesus. Rene challenges us with statements like "It is so easy to love humanity and hate our neighbor" and then reels us in to the kernel of the nutshell:

> " All kinds of pride except honest pride are a result of making it a top priority to look good in the eyes of others as well as ourselves, rather than to love. Love comes from humility. No love in an area means no humility in that area. There is nothing wrong with wanting to look good in our own eyes, and in the eyes of others. It is when we make it more important than love, then it is wrong."

This is a book of reassurance also in those problem areas. Rene faces them head-on and shows us a way to deal with them: "If we have a compulsion, and want to overcome it and don't know how, we shouldn't feel guilty about it. Attempting to do more and try harder won't work. Praying to

Jesus and listening to what He asks us to do is the path to take."

An invaluable book for any reader wanting to grow in their capacity to love.

Anita Patel
Fellow Traveller.

1 INTRODUCTION

My goal in exploring and writing about humility and pride in this book is that I want to love people more deeply, and humility is a key to doing so. I was a very proud person most my life and therefore I was a very poor lover as a result.

Good theology can not by itself change the heart. This book slowly became good theology in my opinion and then began to function sort of like a compass, a North Star, a goal, a hope, together with my book called *Exploring Faith, Hope & Love* in telling me where I wanted to go. But these two books by themselves could not change my many misguided loyalties, bad desires, biases, proud attitudes, meanness, judging, condemning thoughts, and my many other visible sins, and bad energies.

Without confession, repenting in prayer, and renewing the mind the ability to change is minimal at best even with knowledge of what humility looks like. When I say there is "help" in the different contexts in this book I am referring to my book called: *Dismantling the Tree of Knowledge of Good and Evil Within So Love Can Thrive* which explores a path Jesus showed me that leads to personal inner transformation. The books I've written fit together.

This book is about adopting truthful-thinking on how to see God, people, and self with healthy humility, care and compassion. The contents found in this book grew as God led me to true repentance in many areas of my relational life; and that meant because vices were being removed, virtues needed to replace them. Virtues are built up in the heart and mind by believing relational truths that are healthy, non-judgmental and caring.

In order to think in a humble way one needs to stay away from many pitfalls. One's pursuit of humility is not aimed at for one's own sake, but for love's sake. The difference is that the former is like a lady who develops all sorts of techniques to beautify herself but her tongue is toxic and untamed. She will get plenty of looks but her potential at living out healthy relationships is poor until she repents from her toxic tongue. The latter is done by caring for, and becoming compassionate towards people that leads to loving them.

Some of the material covered in this book comes from stuff I struggled with when I was a baby Christian. Back then my intuition said one thing, but the Bible "seemed to say another" or actually did say the opposite. So, this book is also about reconciling these three camps.

The questions wrestled with in this book are as follows:

What are healthy motivations when it comes to doing good deeds? What is the place in one's life of the Old Testament Law, the Moral Law, and the New Testament teachings when it comes to a healthy spiritual life? How are good and evil defined in the Bible, and how is that useful when it comes to judging people? Is it healthier to be in church or out of it? Is there a difference between sin strongholds and what is called the "sin nature" in the Bible? Is there a danger in aiming to be a good person, if so, what is a better motivation? When is boasting wrong? What does it mean for us to let our light shine on others?

What attitudes ought I have when approaching prayer?

Is Jesus' warning to not judge or condemn people still binding on us? Is there a better way than judging people and to still get our concerns across to them? What is the difference between correcting people and judging them? What is an "I" statement? What does it mean to be the salt of the earth?

Are the Beatitudes that Jesus taught still important?

Why choose non-violence as the pathway to peace in the face of conflict? Does non-violence mean doing nothing?

How are legalism and hypocrisy defined and what sorts of dangers can they get us into? Is viewing holiness as spiritual healthiness a key to fending off legalism?

What does it mean to delight in God, so that He will give you the desires of your heart?

What does it mean to abide like a branch in the true Vine: Jesus? What is God's true attitude towards the branches in the Vine? What are the natural loves, and what are their relationships to supernatural love? Why do the branches on the Vine bear good fruit?

What are fitting ways to see oneself and others? What does dependence and independence have to do with humility? Should we be critical of God for how He made us, for what He withholds from us or for what He gives to us? How do the answers to these questions make us treat our neighbors?

Does becoming a Christian means we reject everything from our former way of life? Is there goodness found in other faith traditions? Is an "us vs. them" mentality helpful when it comes to love? Who has the fullness of the truth?

What is the real story behind the dispute between Martha and Mary found in Luke 10? Is forgiveness a license to sin? Why should we forgive?

What is involved in submission to parents, spouses, bosses,

and governments?

Do we worship money and try to use God; or do we use money and worship God?

How does one interpret the Parable of Talents and not get proud?

What does it mean for Jesus to be the way, the truth, and the life?

What does it mean to be born from above or again?

What is Hell about?

What is the true meaning of the Parable of the Prodigal Son? What is rightly directed repentance?

Why did God want Jesus to die for us?

And finally, are we the descendants of Adam and Eve wholly evil, or do we have some goodness in us?

In exploring these questions with the focus being on humility and pride I eventually knew where I wanted my attitudes and actions to take me.

2 MOTIVATING HUMILITY

Let me say from the beginning, that I am no expert when it comes to humility. The contents found in this book have been struggled with, reworked, deleted from, and added to many times over in the years that I have invested in writing it. Which means that it has been a work in progress. I have not attained perfection in how I see humility, but my understanding is continually evolving, getting re-worked, deleted from, and refined over time.

There have been times when the energy within in me was not healthy while writing different parts of this book. But over the years, with the Holy Spirit's help I have edited the book and corrected the unhealthiness within. I do think that this book has something to contribute on humility as it has become sort of like a mirror, a thermometer, and a diagnostic tool meant to help cure me of my different pockets of pride within.

For those who are interested in what I need to say here, I would like to warn you. There are many dangers in attempting to define humility with maxims, lists of do's and don'ts and the like. Conforming to what is said does not mean that one is practicing humility. Knowing what humility is does not mean we are practicing it; we can get proud attitudes because of our knowledge. When one practices humility, then love, peace, and joy are what result, and it does not come from us apart from God, but is done in cooperation with God's grace: His empowering presence in clean and pure energy. God is the one who is glorified.

When one sees mysteries, and connects with them, especially when these mysteries have never entered one's mind before, and one has not ever seemingly heard anyone else utter such things, then one can take on a sense of superiority or a proud attitude because one thinks one is in the know unlike those "other" people. This is a possible danger of being preoccupied with stuff off the beaten path, being a loner, isolating oneself and getting a high off theology (which can be very unhealthy). Spiritual pride is a danger to all of us; that includes those who want to practice humility. So, I need to watch myself.

I do not wish to make people burdened with new lists of sins and to pour on the guilt to somehow motivate good behavior. Rather there is help[1] for uprooting pride once diagnosed and workable recipes for growing humility in us that do lead to love. I'm not into making one struggle more with guilt, shame, or rigid standards in this book. Freedom to love is what I'm after for myself and everyone else.

There is a war that needs to be fought against pride. But only the battles are winnable. The war goes on and on in this valley of shadow of death (this earthly life). Perhaps it goes on in continual victory in Heaven, but it needs to be addressed here on earth. God alone can sustain the victories as we cooperate with Him.

Pride and humility are not "all or nothing" states. Some people have more pride than other people; the key is to not

---

[1] Cf. Rene Lafaut, *Dismantling the Tree of Knowledge of Good and Evil Within So Love Can Thrive*

let pride swallow up the little humility each of us do have.

I heard someone say some time ago that, "he or she who sets themselves up as the sole determiner of or authority on truth only has the gods' laughter." Wanting to be absolutely correct, or too holy is not a good thing to be doing (of which I was guilty of much my adult life). I am not an expert, guru, PhD, priest, or want-to-be pope. Needing others to agree with my slant on truth had been very important to me for a very long time, indeed too important. As if I owned the truth or authored it and needed to somehow be a watchdog or policeman over it.

I can neither give life all by myself nor am I interested in taking anyone else's life. I am no machine, computer, or robot; so, I make mistakes in my thinking about truth and I have moral failures, I take things too seriously at times, I compromise, and I have sinned often. I have also been a perfectionist for a long time; wanting my beliefs to be as clear and truthful as possible as well as lived out. If I can't live out a supposed or real moral, I rightly or wrongly want to jettison that moral and live without it because I hate guilt. I was an "all or nothing"- kind of guy for a long time, but no longer. I don't have it all right, and I am a work in progress.

For most of my past, I have made my cross way too heavy, and in the process also attempted to make other people's crosses way too heavy (please forgive me). I am not perfect, so I can't expect others to be perfect. We all have our own faults. And I want to be as gracious as possible towards others just like I want others to be with me. I have mathematical training, and I love to analyze things way too much instead of letting things be, and accepting them. I love simple truths and principles and I like to meditate on them, and live them out. But life is messy. Linear-correlations are easier to understand and explain than non-linear-correlations. Life and sin is often non-linear; things rapidly escalate into getting messy, knotted, unclear, and confusing a lot of the time because we often don't have clarity to see what is in our hearts or subconscious. Only God knows it all. One can't rest on yesterday's achievements, or limited understanding. Growth calls each of us. We all have some sort of vacuum within our hearts, or restlessness. We all thirst for more. Let's not ignore this and become closed-minded, arrogant, impatient or mean towards those who ask questions we used to ask.

For Christians, there are three standards: The Old Testament Law, the Moral Law, and the New Testament Commands that we can or have struggle(d) with. Living within the Moral Law can be very difficult. The OT Law was an application of the Moral Law for a Jewish culture given a long time ago. When I read the OT Law I see it as a way of trying to make things fair. Wanting things to be fair is healthy, but demanding them with anger, dark mean self-pitying, hostility, abrasiveness, and a "screw-you-attitude" when honor or rights are denied us is not wise or kind. Focusing on having to have things fair all the time often leads to me measuring and judging and trying to avoid losing my lower rights in the process.

But the Commands Jesus put forward in the Sermon on the Mount aim higher than the OT Law, and are only possible to live out with His grace. These Commands of Jesus seek to give more than fairness to those we are called to love. They communicate: I care for you whoever you are to the point of where I'm willing to sacrifice myself and die for you. The commands of Jesus call us to exercise our higher rights to give up our lower rights with gentle, kind, caring, peaceful and humble energy.

When Jesus says that the Ten Commandments still stand, (cf. Matthew 5:17) He is not saying we are under LAW (we are under grace), but that these commandments are still to be used to point out sin. We don't trust in the Ten Commandments to somehow keep the commands. No, we aim higher than these Commandments like the teachings of Jesus and Sermon on the Mount outline. In aiming higher, the OT "minimum standard"[2] will be fulfilled through love prompted through caring and the grace poured out through faith in Jesus.

The OT Law said to not steal or covet; Jesus said to give freely to the poor. The OT Law said don't murder; Jesus said to love our enemies. The OT Law said to sacrifice cattle, bulls and sheep to God; Jesus called us to be living sacrifices. The OT Law said to commit no adultery; Jesus says to love our spouses as ourselves. The OT Law said to not worship lifeless idols, Jesus invited us to true life for free. The OT Law said to honor our parents; Jesus said to take them into our homes,

---

[2] These words were first coined together by Dr. Mark and Patti Virkler in their book *Rivers of Grace* in the context of the OT's importance and is used with permission.

help them, and care for them. The OT Law said to not work on the Sabbath; Jesus said it is healthy to do good on the Sabbath and not be greedy. The OT Law said not to use the Lord's Name in vain; Jesus says we get to call God our Father. The OT Law said, "an eye for an eye, and a tooth for a tooth"[3], but Jesus said use non-violence to spread love. The OT Law said bear no false witnesses; Jesus said to speak the truth in love, believe the best about people, and not to judge or condemn people. The OT Law said to give a percentage; whereas Jesus asks us to be generous just like He is.

So, Jesus' view of the OT Law was to give an even higher standard that when aimed for fulfills the OT Law in the doing without focusing on the OT Law. Jesus raised the standard to an even higher level where God's grace guides, strengthens, blesses, and frees us to love others unconditionally in this new way. Jesus took the "thou shall nots" which are negative and passive in nature, and gave us positive commands that far exceed the OT commands. These commands of Jesus inspire us to positive action, they appeal to our nobleness, they aren't passive in nature, they don't focus on what we are entitled to personally, they don't just limit us to harm reduction but bring health, growth, and help kill selfishness, judging, hostility, pride, and living for pleasure seeking alone.

Jesus promises us that if we abide in Him (humble ourselves in faith) we will bear the good fruit He talked about in the Gospels. But He does not guarantee that we won't sin in this life. He who is without sin may throw the first stone. If we

---

[3] Exodus 21:24

attempt to abide in Him yet still struggle with compulsive sins, then there may be strongholds in our minds or hearts that need to be dealt with. There is help[4] for such problem areas.

I am not better than anyone else; I'd die of embarrassment if all my sins were shown on a BIG screen in front of the whole world. Who am I to judge anyone else? We have all sinned and fallen short of the glory of God; especially me. I do have faith in Jesus, but that does not make me more righteous, humbler, or worthier than other people. All the good I do was and is given to me by God through His blood and sweat and the good I do have I did not earn it. My sins aren't better than anyone else's.

Speaking about right and wrong can often become abstract or self-defeating. Keeping the Sermon on the Mount by foremost rolling up one's sleeves and digging into it with one's own energy isn't wise. We can attempt to keep the Sermon and still miss Jesus along with the people it is intended to protect. It will point to stuff that we don't understand. We need a Shepherd to guide us and intuitively lead us to obey the Sermon when it applies in the many complex and simple situations that arise in life. Love is more than keeping certain rules or laws outwardly; love involves pure motives, energy, and caring attitudes. If we seek to love people, then doing so out of our caring for them is a good motivation. If we focus on the law too much we can invite temptation and can find ourselves in slimy black pits of guilt

---

[4] Cf. Rene Lafaut, *Dismantling the Tree of Knowledge of Good and Evil Within So Love Can Thrive*

feeling powerless and weak. Focusing on good things, pure things, and holy things helps to lessen temptation. The Law makes nothing perfect. Only Jesus makes things perfect. Please keep this in mind while reading this book.

Faith in and relationship with God through Jesus Christ is the only way to love "supernaturally" for those who have heard the Good News of Jesus Christ and understood it. There is no principle, code, system, technique, or motive that can produce love all by itself. Jesus is the true Vine, and no matter what others say, you may be able to do "natural" good without being in relationship with Him, but you can't love supernaturally without being in relationship with Him if you have heard the Good News and understood it. I want authentic love and no cheap imitation. In me learning how to love I have been broken repeatedly.

If there is any truth in this book on "humility" then I know that no Christian can practice it authentically unless they are guided and energized by Jesus with healthy beliefs. This is made possible through faith in, trust in, prayer to, and relationship with God. There are many dangers in describing what humility looks like. Only God can see directly into the hearts of people, and we often don't know our own hearts or motives in the first place, hence the need to hear what God has to say personally to each of us about it.

Practicing humility by focusing on ourselves and exclusively on lists of do's and don'ts is doomed to failure and leads to trying to conform instead of being transformed. The more we focus on ourselves the more we will be tempted to get proud because of our success, or deflated, guilty, and downcast because of our failures. Love isn't about me, myself, my reputation, how I look, and what I get out of it. The more we try to correct our bad behavior by ourselves (through pressure or pushing stuff down within) to conform to LAW, the more we will lose sight of Jesus. When we lose sight of Jesus the more we will feel angry pressure, self-pity, guilt, impatience, and judgment directed towards others and ourselves. We were never intended to correct our behaviors by lonesome selves. That is God's job because He is the one who made us from the inside out.

It is important to search for truth, but it is just as important to ask why one is searching for truth. Put another way: pursuing truth (or right behavior) is important, but the reasons for why I am pursuing truth (or right behavior) are just as important. Seekers of truth won't necessarily find love; whereas seekers of love will find truth. A friend of mine with whom I have corresponded with on this topic explains some of these dangers regarding this subject, and that I happen to agree with:

> The term I should have used was "moralism" - a religious first cousin of legalism - which I understand to be the pursuit of righteousness through the doing of "good works". And here Paul and Jesus make it clear that our righteousness is not derived directly from good works, but only as an outworking of God's work through Jesus and in transforming us by His Spirit. Moralism also involves succumbing to the temptation

(often unconscious) of believing that if I do this good thing, and that good thing like it says in the Bible (and of course Paul provides many such lists of "goods") then all will be well. The danger here is that a person places their faith in their own power to do good, and then also the danger of becoming self-righteous and judging oneself to be superior to others who do not do all or as many of the same acts. I understand the Jesus way to involve the transformation/ purification of the heart, which then leads the person to do those good works, not because of what you "get" for them (salvation or otherwise), but simply because they are good. You don't "think/analyze" whether it fits God's law - you just do it because that is who you are [in Christ]. Only God is truly "good" - but as we become more in love with Him, our being is changed and we act more like he would act.

There is so much to chew on here. Going to the Torah (OT Law) or Moral Law every time we fail in keeping it and holding onto the Torah more tightly inside our hearts trying to keep the Torah (OT Law) or Moral Law is not wise. The Torah (OT Law) and Moral Law are intended to point out sin. They have no power by themselves to make us obey God. Guilt should drive us to God and not directly to doing good deeds. Being transformed by God's Love (the Holy Spirit) through faith, and relationship with Him is the wisest path to take to grow in supernatural Love. It is the only path to supernatural Love. Doing good deeds (prescribed by the Law (Torah, or Moral) or some other systems of principles) with the hope of getting

Salvation, points of merit, badges of righteousness, favor from God, or the favor of our peers goes against the Spirit of Love. When we love for love's sake then we truly love God. Whenever we aim to get something out of the good works we are doing other than just loving people with those good works, then we are off course.

If we sin, then we don't do more or try harder to stay away from that sin. We learn to rest in God's promises concerning our salvation from sin when we learn to confess our sins to God, and become consciously dependent on Him in faith so He can purify us from the sins we commit[5]. Often, we commit sins because we have believed, and think lies or half-truths. Often, we commit sins because we aren't dependent on God's grace. Often, we commit sin because we aren't teachable. Us having resentments, fears, and pride in our lives are pathways to committing compulsive sins too.

Fear is a root to sin because it leads to holding onto whatever is close by to achieve a goal so that we become independent from God (i.e. proud) and so become self-made men and women instead of becoming God's workmanship.

When we love God or any other person, then we don't want to harm, hurt, or offend them; we want to bless them. When we love, we become sensitive towards those we love. When we love, it is because we care for those we love.

When we break the least commandment, we are guilty of breaking the whole Law: which is to love; because the whole

---

[5] Cf. 1 John 1:9

law can be summarized in: love God, neighbor, and self.

When we hold onto God's Love we will want to, and will move towards loving others. When we hold onto serious sin then we can't embrace God's love until we come to Him and throw ourselves at His mercy, grace, wisdom, and power to pry us loose from our serious sins. "We can't serve two masters: We will either hate one or love the other".[6]

As Christians, we are called to no longer lead a sinful life. Not sinning means the Moral Law is binding on us. But aiming to not sin using the Moral Law as the means to not sin won't get us anywhere. A simple stone keeps all the Ten Commandments perfectly. But that stone by itself can't dispense mercy. We are called to a higher goal: active love, the way Jesus taught and showed. If we focus on following and loving Jesus wherever we meet Him, then we will immediately fulfill the requirements from the Moral Law . But if we focus on "not sinning" then we will be Law focused and get nowhere fast.

God calls us to a love-relationship, not a fear-driven-slave-mentality-relationship. He wants us to move from "fear of making him angry when we do wrong" to "caring for Him and what he wants". He doesn't want us to be insecure, and not aware that we are loved by Him. God's love eventually results in peace, joy, and love for those who commit to following His only Eternally begotten Son: Jesus.

Concerning one's motivation to live out goodness, the

[6] Luke 16:13

following questions can be asked:

(1) Does me saying and believing: "I must keep God's commandments because of what I think I'll get (Heaven) and not get (Hell)" lead to pressure and that pressure lead to either failure (i.e. guilt) or pride (i.e. self-righteousness), or does it get the job done?

(2) Does me saying and believing, "I want to keep God's commandments because God first loves me (as shown on the cross)" lead to me bearing good fruit and that more abundantly or is it just wishful thinking?

I think that the answer to question (1) from my own experience has been: "failure (i.e. guilt) or pride (i.e. self-righteousness).

And I think the answer to question (2) is that it leads to bearing good fruit.

If we leave God out of our equations in doing good works, then we get in danger of becoming self-righteous. Self-righteousness says: "I can keep the commandments because I am the source of my own goodness." Self-righteousness can also wrongly say: "I keep certain rules and in doing so I have peace and so gain acceptance with God". In doing so one will be saying that God's love is not good enough, or the work of Jesus on the cross is not good enough. Ultimately one is dependent on God for all things especially the grace or power and leading in loving others. But we can also claim to be dependent on God and do many good works, but fall because we judge others to be not as good or as holy or as pure as we see ourselves. Preaching, teaching, and living out morality are very tricky things.

What I have written in this book is the result of valuable dialogue that I have had over the years with a variety of people from many different backgrounds. I am thankful to those who stood up to me, and so helped correct so many (not all) of the errors I had and have concerning my understanding of humility. It is also the result of my search for love, because without humility there can be no wholesome love. I guess that humility at its foundation or roots is partially about motives. Like a Priest said to me, "each fallen human heart is like a gigantic mine field." There will always be battles with bad motives before we enter Heaven and the beatific vision.

Much of what I have written may seem moralistic, or too absolute. I have written about how I view humility from the perspectives I have been exposed to (South African, Canadian, European, American; Protestant and Catholic for the most part), in a certain time or era. Years from now what I have written may seem like nonsense by those who read it. This points to the truth that humility looks different on the outside (from culture to culture and from time to time), but on the inside, it does not change or contradict itself because it has to do with motives, health, energy, mechanics, and peace.

I have many times misunderstood the Sermon on the Mount, and will continue to do this until death. Like I said, I started out writing this book because I thought I had something to contribute to interpreting the Moral Law as given by Jesus in the Sermon on the Mount. We all do, yet life isn't about pushing the envelope on moral systems of behavior, it is about living out love because we are caring for people.

A long while ago, I was flipping channels on my TV when I tuned into two Rabbis discussing the OT Law or Jewish Torah. One of them made the comment that if all we are doing is trying to love others because God commands us then we can't have too high an opinion about those we are attempting to love. This confused me. But then gradually I began to see that God commands us to love each other because He made each of us in His image. And God's image is nothing but goodness. So, when we agree with God and decide to love our neighbor, it is because our neighbor is worth it. If we don't care for our neighbor we can't or won't love them. God is Light, and so exposes things for what they are. God loves us, and He desires us to partake in His kind of Love.

Most people want to love in a way that suits themselves, but God wants us to love according to His nature, will, and desires because His ways are always healthy, unlike our ways. God's thoughts are as high as the heavens are above the earth compared to our ways.

Perhaps what you will find here is nonsense. Perhaps it is enlightened in some areas. I have made a lot of mistakes in my Christian life. I still have struggles. There is still tension in my thinking. Perhaps that is the power of paradox. Perhaps it is because of my blindness.

3 GROWING IN HUMILITY AND DYING TO PRIDE

The Old Testament uses the words "good" and "evil" in this sense: "good" is "functional": doing what it was designed to do by God; whereas "evil" is "dysfunctional": being used for an inappropriate end in God's eyes. So, in some sense evil is a spiritual disease infecting something good, whereas good is spiritual health.

Christians use the word evil to mean a shortage or lacking or eating away from the good present. Therefore, evil can't exist on its own. It needs to warp or blemish or infect or make sick something good for it to exist. Just like rust does to cars or rotten-ness does to apples.

Therefore, the thinking that most promotes humility, is thinking of spiritual growth as getting healthy; and sin as being unhealthy. The problem with seeing growth as getting "better or improving" is that it opens the door to comparisons ("before vs. after" or "me vs. others") too easily. We are all sick or unhealthy spiritually in different ways, so comparisons are fruitless: Comparisons can easily lead to envy or pride. You can't compare oranges with apples or pears. Moreover, when health comes to a patient the doctor should get the credit. Likewise: Jesus is our spiritual doctor[7]. He should get the credit for bringing health to our souls.

Some people think that by withdrawing affection, warmth,

---

[7] Cf. Mark 2:17

and kindness from a "sinner", that they can show disapproval of the sinner's life choices or behaviors, and somehow shame the "sinner" to correct the behavior. This does not work. The "sinner" this is aimed at often thinks there is something wrong with the person who acts like this towards them. This strategy neglects the truth that we all sin, and that we all have flaws in our natures. In pointing a finger at the one we want to "repent"; three fingers are pointing back to us. We can't change anyone; focusing on ourselves is wiser, and is non judgmental. When we love we inspire people; when we try to fix them they feel judged, and get defensive. It is God's kindness that leads to us changing our ways; not threats, pressure, shame, demands, or karma.

In the World, or in the Church?

If one thinks one can escape the temptations from the world by entering the church one is blindsided. The church will offer its own set of temptations. Sometimes we are healthier in our beliefs just before we enter the church, and get spiritually more ill by entering the church. Put more precisely, we take our baggage with us wherever we go. There are all sorts of spiritual viruses in the world and in the church. Holiness is not a result of any virus. It is the fruit of a humble faith or properly building on a healthy foundation. We have all sorts of attitudes that evolve, morph, or grow in many environments. In this context: either the church or the world.

There is a difference between a "sin stronghold" and what is called our "sin nature". The former can be dismantled whereas the latter can't be crucified, killed, or destroyed by us. Knowing this simplifies the battles we ought to fight.

The strongholds of sin are what I call "the tree of knowledge of good and evil" within us, whose seed, structure and fruit has infected all fallen humanity: Adam and Eve and us their fallen descendants. The tree's infecting power is in the lies spoken to us that we too quickly and easily embrace because they promise us instant peace, alleviation of fears, and the lie that God's promises to provide ways through difficulties are not trustworthy. The devil promised independence, and made us slaves to sin, but only Jesus can free us from this tangled mess through the Good News found in the New Testament (NT).

When one lives according to the Torah or OT LAW, and measures oneself by it, trying to use it to be righteous, then the focus is on oneself and rules; and pride will be the natural outcome if one is successful. But when we abide in the true Vine – Jesus, then the focus won't be on us, and we won't attempt to conform to what humility looks like by our own efforts. Instead we will begin to supernaturally love and find joy in Jesus because He is the true joy for those who discover His beauty. We will when we patiently await it, be transformed by God into vessels of His love.

When we have an ideal that we aim for like being a certain type of woman or man, we must be careful, that our focus is not to fit a certain mold, instead of caring for or being concerned for those people we meet on our path each day. It is so easy to love humanity, and hate our neighbor. Humble people care for those who cross their paths, whereas proud people are more concerned about fitting a certain mold they deem as perfection and are less concerned about others than the way they themselves look. People who attempt to conform to an ideal such as only being a good person in the eyes of others will usually only do good when in the presence of or when seen by others. When I read the Gospels, I find Jesus loving whomever crossed His path: sinners, people of bad reputations, those seen as burdens such as disabled people, those in need, those who were hungry for food, peace, acceptance, love, meaning and joy. Jesus did not make it His top priority to look good, respectable, and acceptable. He refused to be boxed in, and that was hard to accept by those who did not understand Him. He did not aim at perfection; He was perfection. I know that my spiritual journey picked up steam when I concluded that I needed to meet others where they are at in my own small way just like Jesus did.

All kinds of pride except honest pride are a result of making it our top priority to look good in the eyes of others as well as ourselves, rather than to love. Love comes from humility. No love in an area means no humility in that area.

When we make our main goal to love others like the Sermon on the Mount outlines, then it doesn't mean that we necessarily have humility.[8] The Old Testament Law was an application of the Moral Law for the times, circumstances, customs, and culture inherited by Abraham's descendants after an exodus from slavery in Egypt. Some of the Jews

---

[8] Cf. Matthew 5:1-7:29, or Luke 6:20-6:49

during Jesus' earthly ministry pored over that same Law thinking that in them they would have life, but they persecuted Jesus the author of life and the Law. They had the outward appearance of righteousness but denied the power and way to keep the spirit of the law. We can do the same thing with the Sermon on the Mount.

Humility is not an all or nothing thing. All people have different degrees of humility. We can squander it in one area, or grow it in another, depending on our choices.

When someone practices humility they are willing to look bad when they are doing good. They are willing to listen to and follow other people who are practicing humility. Humble people are aware of their pride. They are aware of their pride because they allow the true light that is coming into the world to expose their pride for what it is. Humble people hate their pride. By hate I mean these people have the tendency to not want to give themselves over to it.

Proud people want to look good at all costs. And so, they will be tempted to try to make others look bad in an attempt to look good themselves. When one thinks one looks good when in fact one looks anything but good, one must be blind. The darkness has made one blind.

There is nothing wrong with wanting to look good in our own eyes, and in the eyes of others. It is when we make it more important than love, then it is wrong.

When Is Boasting Wrong?

It is always important to attempt to speak what we believe to be the truth because that is part of what it means to be humble. But sometimes we should refrain from speaking the truth about what we do, because otherwise we are becoming proud.

Sometimes when I watch TV, I see certain businesses advertise the supposed good their companies are doing for certain charities. And I think that they do so from mixed motives. The heads of these companies either never read the words of Jesus (below) or misunderstand them, or aren't wise enough to follow them. Jesus said:

> A city on a hill cannot be hidden. Neither do people light a lamp and put it under a bowl. Instead they put it on its stand, and it gives light to everyone in the house. In the same way, *let your light shine before men*, that they may see your good deeds and praise your Father in heaven.[9]

Do the italicized words in this quotation mean that we are to broadcast to everyone: "Hey look at the good I did or am doing for this person or those persons" when we do an act of kindness? I don't think so. Motives and focus are important.

Having said this there is another side to this topic. Mother Theresa got into the public eye with her tangible love, but her motives had nothing to do with making a name for herself. Her example was very good when it came to caring for people despite the fact that she was not perfect.

Good deeds aren't always the same as love. Good deeds that

---

[9] Matthew 5:14-16, (emphasis mine)

are done with right motives, energy, and mechanics are considered love in God's eyes. When people have ulterior motives in doing good deeds then those deeds no matter how good, are not fully love. The only thing that counts is faith working itself out into love.

Those businesses that give to good causes because it is merely good business may be both proud and greedy. They may want to look good in the public eye only to earn greater profits. Their bottom line is helping others out only because it is profitable and they look good doing so. When humility acts, the result is love.

Having said this, I think that the heads of certain companies aren't the only ones at fault. We may all at different times be guilty of something very similar. We do this when we give money away because we don't want to look bad, or because we want to look good, even when there is no monetary profit in it for us. People who give alms because they want to look humble are proud. They are more interested in appearances than loving people. The path to love is caring for people and not attempting to conform to a concept or ideal.

There are times when it is prudent to let others know that we give, because when we do, we are not trying to boast. This may occur when someone asks us to defend our integrity when it comes to doing stuff for the poor. Or, when we are trying to teach our children to give. But we must watch the motives and energies in our hearts, lest we give way to more pride in our hearts.

So, how do we interpret the above words by Jesus? I think

that they ought to be interpreted this way. Light is a metaphor for love. When we let our light shine on a group of people, it is because we are loving each member from the group individually. And the reason each person may know about it is because we have loved her or him in a caring way. They in turn might tell others what we did, but that is different than seeking to glorify ourselves. When we dislike someone, who crosses our path we ought not cover our light (our love) with a bowl and make that person walk in our darkness: Love calls us to love everyone who we meet no matter how difficult it may be or get. Our light ought to shine on those people whose paths we cross.

Boasting about almsgiving is always wrong. Only the shallow will do it.

Almsgiving is not the only event where we should watch out for wrong motives. When we pray or fast Jesus warned us that we should watch the motives and focus in our hearts too.

There is nothing wrong with public prayer per-se. Even Jesus prayed when He was around others on occasions. It is when we are praying only to look good in other people's eyes, and not because we are concerned for those we are praying for, that our motives are wrong. God doesn't hear prayers that are motivated by vanity. The only people we impress are those with a poor understanding of humility, and those who would most likely do the same.

There are other times when people might find out we are praying. This may occur when we wish to encourage and hearten a person going through a difficult time by telling them we are praying for them ourselves. If this is done correctly then we are not doing so to boast, but to give hope and life. Our motives are important.

When we boast about our fasting then we have spiritual pride. Jesus said that we have our reward already if we make an effort to reveal the fact that we are fasting. When we are fasting for the right reasons, it is because we want to be close to God, want to make room for Him, seek direction from Him, or want to show our solidarity with those who are less fortunate. Motives and mechanics are important when one decides whether an act is being done out of humility or pride.

4 PRAYING THE LORD'S PRAYER

For those who aren't familiar with the Lord's Prayer, here it is:

Our Father in heaven,
hallowed be your name,
your kingdom come,
your will be done on earth as it is in heaven.
Give us today our daily bread.
Forgive us our debts,
as we also have forgiven our debtors.
And lead us not into temptation,
but deliver us from the evil one.[10]

When we are spiritually proud in an area we can resemble the father of lies more than we do God the Father in the area. When we are blind to our pride, we may think that God is just like we are, and so call Him Father. When we do this, it has nothing to do with having been adopted into His family through faith, mercy and grace. If we were adopted, we have possibly temporarily forgotten it.

Living out, "hallowed be your name" to God is more difficult than it may appear. Our actions should bring His name glory. We all suffer from pride in degrees and so in different ways covet the glory belonging to God in our own hearts, and so it may seem that we can't possibly mean these words in their truest sense in prayer. But we pray the prayer out of our poverty, not riches, and not only for others but for ourselves

---

[10] Matthew 6:9-13

too. We don't have to be perfect to pray the Lord's Prayer. We pray because we know our poverty, our need, and our desire. We also pray because we know our faults, imperfections, and guilt. We pray because we may truly desire to be holy in our thoughts, words, and actions even when they are not so. We pray, "hallowed be your Name" to God because it in part helps sustain the little humility we do have. When we truly praise God, we start knowing our place and are on our way to freedom.

The Bible says that God knows the arrogant and proud of heart from afar (because the proud and arrogant usually push Him away). It is hard to get close to a proud person because they are so full of themselves. But many proud people can and do search for God. Proud people can be blind to their pride and God knows that. We don't clean ourselves up to get into God's presence; we go to Him and He cleans us up; it is a process to get clean and pride also needs to be cleaned up. When we pray for God's Kingdom to come, we are inviting God's presence into our lives. People who are acting out their pride are too busy competing with others, and so, if God were to show up, they would compete with God. Proud people dislike it when others more glorious than themselves show them up. I know in the past that I have been envious of those who I deemed to be more popular or manly than myself.

When we compete to the point of hating our rivals, then we need to learn how to mean and desire the words, "your kingdom come" when directed to God. The proud are more than likely going to pray this to themselves; but even the proud do have consciences and so can recognize their fallen-ness and so pray this to God. Only the truly blind, those with darkened consciences will have difficulty praying this.

At different times, we all think that we know better than God about our circumstances and what He has to say in the Gospels, so if we do pray, "your will be done on earth as it is in heaven" to God we may be blind to what God's Kingdom is about. But who knows better that God's will needs to be done and want to pray it than those who struggle with doing God's will? No matter how far we have transgressed, God desires for us to pray these words. We don't have to be super-ultra-pure to be able to utter these words to God. And that is the Good News: God welcomes us to walk with Him no matter where we are in this life. We not only pray that we will do God's will, but we pray that everyone will do likewise. In praying this we need to be careful to not demand (i.e. meanly expect) it from anyone else. We are not moral police. We pray God's will be done so that even when others don't do it, we won't get critical, self-righteously judgmental, angry, mean, condemning, hard hearted, and cold towards them.

Perfect love puts no limits on what I am to do concerning God's spoken will to me. But who has perfect love? If I want to love, then it isn't wise to limit what I know God expects from me. Praying the Lord's Prayer where it says: "Your will [oh God] be done on earth as it is in Heaven" means that I shouldn't hold anything back from God that God wants me to give. I shouldn't say, "I'll only do so much of God's will", but on the other hand I'm not perfect in love, and God is not anal.

The Lord's Prayer is a call to approach over time total commitment to God and His will. Gradual growth in commitment is best. Giving up beliefs and judgments that are contrary to what God is telling us through the Scriptures, wholesome church community, and His Spirit is key to building up commitment because the process will bear good fruit. Such a process is called Inner Transformation.

Holding back from caring for others will mean we are acting out our selfishness. Selfishness comes from our desire to have it all. When we care for others we will carry their burdens in prayer to God. Such sympathy is not burdensome, because we aren't left holding burden after burden without relief. Giving our burdens to Jesus at the cross frees us to move on in life and to retain our joy in the journey.

Proud people are more than likely going to take or demand their daily bread, than humbly ask for and receive it from God. The bread talked about here also means God's grace (His empowering presence) which comes from His unconditional love.

After Jesus taught His disciples to pray the above words with meaning. He warned them that if they refused to forgive those people who sinned against them, God might not hear their prayers. Proud, arrogant, merciless and heartless people won't forgive when they are aware of un-forgiveness in their hearts. That doesn't mean that people who need to forgive and want to forgive will forgive. Many don't know how to forgive.

I heard one radio evangelist preach what he considered and

claimed to be the pure unadulterated Gospel of Christ. But on one of his shows he had to admit that he didn't know how to show others how to forgive when they wanted to but didn't know how. If all you have is theory, then you have never fully practiced what you preach. And, therefore perhaps, the theory is quite possibly wrong or incomplete. No wonder many in the church are weak and not growing in their faith.

In the book: *Going Deeper With The Twelve Steps* I show one how to forgive. Everyone should know this, especially those who claim to be servants of the Gospel. Forgiveness is at the very heart of the Gospel.

Depending on just how proud a person becomes, they might think that they are invincible. Humble people are aware of the wickedness in their own hearts, and tremble knowing what the future might bring as far as temptation is concerned. So, they willingly pray the last two lines from the Lord's Prayer. True, they will have some confidence in God's good will towards them, but they also know that two people walk together only while they are agreed.

5 WHEN IS JUDGING POMPOUS OR NOT?

The context in which I am using the word, "judging" here is as follows:

> I am "Judging" another person when I give my opinion about them, or I pass a sentence on them that either puts them down, insults them, boxes them in, or hurts them.

I might do this because I don't know how to speak the truth in a way that makes known what I want without hurting them. Judging often leads to despising (refusing to love) the person because of his or her behaviors and/or beliefs based on certain criteria (usually the supposed superiority of my beliefs, or my conduct). Judging leads to despising a person because they refuse to comply with one's wishes.

The road to love in my life eventually challenged my stubborn self-righteous, blind, judgmental, angry, and self-pitying, hypocritical mean attitudes by not taking to heart Jesus' statement:

> Do not judge, or you too will be judged. For in the same way as you judge others, you will be judged, and with the measure you use, it will be measured to you.[11]

In other parts of Scripture, Jesus says that we should judge for ourselves, and not by appearances.[12] Is Jesus

---

[11] Matthew 7:1-2
[12] Cf. Luke 12:57, & John 7:24

contradicting Himself here, or does what He is saying go deeper? It goes deeper! There is judging between truth and falsehoods which is acceptable, but the act of judging any person is forbidden.

So how do we not judge a person, but at the same time let the person know we are being hurt or are upset? What is the difference between judging and making one's point of view known? What is the best way to define it?

Judging involves measuring and estimating and marking someone up with a label that hits home because we are trying to control or change them, or make them guilty so they will change. Judging is not like telling the truth. Judging is telling someone else about what I think about them. Whereas telling the truth is about telling something about myself honestly."[13] The former is all opinion, or speculation, or casts a bad light on somebody else, it brings fear, it brings hurt, it is not gentle and puts people on the defensive. Judging always creates distance. Telling the truth is about how I see myself, and so is authoritative when honest.

So, when somebody hurts us, and we don't want to judge, then we won't speculate on his or her motives or intent, or supposed stupidity, or abrasiveness, or his or her lack of kindness, or his or her pride and arrogance, or his or her weaknesses and tell him or her so. If we are hurt by them, then telling them how we feel and how we are struggling to handle what is happening inside of us is telling the truth.

---

[13] Danny Silk, used with permission.

Telling the truth uses "I" statements and does not blame or point the finger. Telling the truth appeals to another person's noble ness, humanness, warmth, kindness, and caring. It doesn't try to convict, shame, blame, or disrespect; and put the person on the defensive, make them want to hurt us back and want to judge us back. Judging robs the person of self-esteem, self-worth, honor, and respect.

An "I" statement has the following structure:

"I feel "_____" when "_____" because "_____",
and would like "_____"

it is non-judgmental, it is not offensive, it does not attack, but respects boundaries, reputations, and the dignity of people. It is not coercive but appeals to the nobility of people instead.

No one rejoices over judging; but because of truth's nature those who seek truth rejoice over truth.[14]

In me judging, I harden my heart, and make my tongue toxic. But truth can lead to sympathy, empathy, compassion, kindness, change, and mutual respect; it gives the benefit of the doubt, it believes the best about people[15]. Judging can believe and accuse people of the worst.

The reason why we are very sorely tempted into thinking judgmental thoughts and to want to follow through on judging is because we feel injustices have been visited on us. Even when we recognize that Jesus commands us to not judge, we are pulled this way to try to make things right

---

[14] First Corinthians 13:6
[15] First Corinthians 13:7

because we think that if we don't speak up things will get worse. This tension occurs because we don't know how to speak our truth gently. Judging attacks whereas speaking the truth does not. Truth speaking involves using "I" statements and owning our feelings in conversation with those who hurt us and is more likely to illicit understanding and change (although those who don't care may laugh us off) whereas, when we judge, then we blame and put people on the defensive.

Years ago, I was promised an opportunity that was not coming through for me. I was tempted to get bitter, hostile, and I had many judgmental thoughts towards the person I thought was responsible for reneging on his promise. But when it came time to confront the person I did not blame him, I said how I felt, I did not vent, hate, scream injustice, or judge the person. A few days later the opportunity came my way. I now know the person did not feel judged by me, and he was warmed by my response to his cold shoulder. I see this as a powerful example of the difference between judging and telling the truth.

Remembering the many consequences of judging along with what judging is and what truth telling are will help one to stay away from judging. But there is a lot more to it than just this.

Jesus gave a rule or condition under which one person is allowed to correct or help another person out of a sin.

> Why do you see the speck of sawdust in your brother's eye, and pay no attention to the plank in your own eye? How can you say to your brother, 'Let me take

the speck out of your eye,' when all the time there is the plank in your own eye? You hypocrite, first take the plank out of your own eye, and then you will see clearly to remove the speck out of your brother's eye.[16]

As Christians, we ought not think the sin that one's brother or sister commits won't ever be a problem for us. Scripture is clear that we need to watch ourselves lest we fall. There go I but for the grace of God. Speaking from experience, I know that it is very easy to get angry with someone when they attempt to correct me in some area. If we do fulfill the requirement mentioned above (i.e. not being a hypocrite) by Jesus and attempt to help remove a speck from our brother or sister's eye, then we need to "be as wise as serpents and as innocent as doves."[17] By brother or sister, I mean someone who professes to follow Jesus Christ.

I think the above condition applies to three situations.

(1) That is, the sin committed involves both of us. It is our personal business. As stated above, using "I" statements is the healthiest thing to do because it is truth telling and not loaded with blame or judgments.

(2) When the situation does not involve us, then we don't have the leverage, right, or ability to speak the truth unless invited by the person who needs correction.

(3) The person is off their rocker and just hurt someone, or

---

[16] Matthew 7:3-5
[17] Cf. Matthew 10:16

almost just hurt someone , or will hurt someone badly.

When an unbeliever does an unholy act, then we need to be careful that we don't judge them in our hearts or with our mouths. If they invite our opinion, then we can give it. If they aren't interested in our opinions then Jesus said:

> Do not give dogs what is sacred; do not throw your pearls to pigs, if you do, they may trample them under their feet and turn and tear you to pieces.[18]

I've felt justified in my sins many times. I know how it can feel when one is blind to a sin, and someone points it out (even) lovingly. One may think, "Who is this stiff-necked hypocrite? And why is he telling me that this precious gift is wrong? Why did he ever show up? He just wants to spoil the fun!"

As a Christian, I am not called to regulate, change, control, force, or manipulate others (Christian or non-Christian alike) into seeing and doing things the Christian way. The only person I can change is myself if at all. If we have the idea that, "we only need to hit others over the head with enough truth (or with what we rightly or wrongly think is truth (or salt[19])) to make them see and do things our way," then we need to abandon the idea.

It is true that Jesus had some very sad and upsetting things to say about certain segments of the Jewish population of His time. He had a right to point out their sins because He is God, and the Judge of the world; also, He is neither a hypocrite,

---

[18] Matthew 7:6
[19] Cf. Matthew 5:13

self-righteous in a bad way (i.e. proud), nor a slanderer. He said it in love, not meanness, not hatefully, not hostilely, not judgmentally, not hardening His heart, not to hurt the people, not to slap them in the face, and not to feel superior to them. He also said these things as a warning to us, and not to make those He judged to necessarily look bad; they already did. Just because we claim to be following Jesus doesn't mean that all the things He did we can necessarily do. We can't walk ahead of Jesus and think presumptuously that He would do this or that. Just because Jesus accepts worship doesn't mean we can. Just because Jesus walked on water doesn't mean that we can. Just because He pointed out wrongs from others (followers and non-followers alike) doesn't mean that we can pass judgments like He did. Jesus attempted to correct in healthy ways and He had no speck or timber in His eyes. Jesus forbids judging and condemning in the Gospels. We need to take this to heart.

Humility longs for correction, because love is its objective. No one really likes to be corrected: both the proud and the humble, because we all have some unhealthy pride. Correction can feel humiliating, especially if we are conceited.

Every person can become a lesson in humility for us. That does not mean a lesson in humiliation. I do mean that we can learn stuff from almost anyone. Their consciences may be clearer in certain areas than are ours, even if they are not a believer in Jesus.

I used to think that if there is a judgment on the last day, then it was a good thing to warn anyone (Christian, or non-

Christian alike) who is committing certain moral wrongs to repent from them. I saw my judging or pointing out their sin as an opportunity to share the Gospel – boy was I ever deluded.[20]

But now I'm in touch with the truth that I'm not a moral policeman, and more, I don't have the moral authority to go about correcting people. When I step into a situation that is not my business, and begin to judge, I am going to get anger coming my way. And likely bring the way of Jesus into disrepute. God has written the moral law on each person's heart – can we do any better?

If we see that a person is feeling guilty then we can share the Good News of God's forgiveness with them if we are invited to. If someone asks me whether I think that certain acts are right or wrong, then I am allowed to give my opinion. If someone wants to debate a certain issue in a humane way, then there is nothing wrong with putting forth arguments in love to win over an opponent and learn from them. But if we are wrong then the wise and prudent thing is to admit it. And if we aren't making an effort to change our own conduct, then how can anyone take us seriously on moral issues or opinions. Christians are called to be both salt and light in this world.[21]

I was told a long time ago that salt is used to keep meat from decaying. From this I thought that Christians were called to

---

[20] I am grateful to Marilyn for showing me the stupidity of this position.
[21] Cf. Matthew 5:13

keep society from decaying morally by plastering the people with as many truthful morals or as much salt as possible so that they would not decay morally. I now realize that plastering others with plenty of morals, and rules may stop them from decaying morally but it won't give them life. They might try to conform to the morality, but what they really need is inner-transformation.

When Jesus calls us to be salt He means that we are to get others in touch with their thirst for God and love, and when they get in touch with this thirst they will want to drink the living water (God) and He will give them life. If we can submit to God in such a way as to let Christ shine through us, then others will be drawn to Christ and His way of loving others through us. This is much more effective than hitting people over the head with "so-called truth", "moralizing", or "mounds of salt" or "our judgments" or "preaching" hoping that they will eventually somehow believe out of shame or guilt. People feel guilty enough.

When we judge others, it means that we have become faultfinders. "Love covers a multitude of sins."[22] We weren't sent into the world to morally police others by pointing out their faults (they probably know about them already). People respond to holy (healthy) examples better than preaching. When others ask why we are honest instead of cheating, giving instead of greedy, and loving instead of resentful, then we can share our pearls or holy things with them. This is what

---

[22] 1 Peter 4:8

Jesus meant by:

> "Do not give dogs what is sacred; do not throw your
> pearls to pigs. If you do they will trample them under
> their feet and turn and tear you to pieces."[23]

If we do share our pearls with those who didn't ask for them
then they might trample those truths and maul us. We need
to wait for permission to share our wisdom. We can't rush
into things. Love is patient, kind and tolerant.

We should make it a regular practice to humbly pray for those
who we disagree with on moral matters. It may change them,
but will foster more love in our hearts towards them if we
want to love and not so much be right. We all have at least a
few hundred things wrong within us so we should choose our
battles wisely. We aren't called to be "moral" policemen. The
attitude: "there go I but for the grace of God" is what we
should aim for.

If you ever get tested in severe trials, you will come to know
what is in your heart. It is amazing how quick we might be to
judge God's commands as indispensable in certain instances,
and not so in others. One moment we might expound on the
glory of Jesus, and how wonderful it is to follow in His ways.
While the next moment we may feel that His sayings are too
hard, idealistic, don't apply, or are too uncompromising when
we are tested. What used to be sweet may become bitter for
a while (or forever). Love requires us to sacrifice the very
parts of ourselves that are selfish, pampered, and proud.

---

[23] Matthew 7:6

Humility hungers for right living, first in our own lives and then in other people's lives. Jesus said, "Blessed are those who hunger and thirst for righteousness, for they will be filled".[24]

---

[24] Matthew 5:6

6 SOME BEATITUDES

Jesus said in the Gospel of Matthew: "Blessed are the meek for they will inherit the earth"[25]. If we go about angrily and meanly demanding our rights from others and they don't come through then we will get judgmental, and resentful. In fact, being meanly demanding is always done with bad energy and we need to confess it and repent in prayer from it in all the contexts where it is found in our relationships. If we attempt to grasp what we think we deserve and don't treat others the ways we want to be treated, then we are acting out of pride and selfishness. Those who are meek (slow to anger, gentle and unselfish) will not meanly demand their rights. They will invoke a higher right to give up a lower right when it comes to that. This can't be done in one's own energy, but only through prayer and yielding to God's will in this context. The meek might not get plenty of real estate or respect now, but Jesus has promised that they will get real estate after they die. The proud and arrogant will take what they think they deserve. The humble will give even when it hurts.

The kind of wisdom offered by "the tree of knowledge of good and evil" in the Garden of Eden was Carnal. It was earthly, and demonic because it replaced God as the final authority on right and wrong. It was the kind of knowledge that has to do with getting one's own way and using others to get it. Such a kind of wisdom goes against meekness. God

---

[25] Matthew 5:5

knew about this kind of knowledge all along, but because of His purity He is never tempted to embrace it. We on the other hand have it living in us: it is the result of our wills and desires not being completely in sync with the healthy life of God. The only remedy is a relationship with God through Jesus Christ that embraces the life God offers and to reject our own supposed "godhood".

Another Beatitude Explained:

Jesus said in the Gospel of Matthew: "Blessed are you who mourn for you will be comforted."[26] Those people who get judgmental, mean and angry towards people who are living a life of immoral pleasures or sin do so out of pride and don't care for those they call sinners. They have become self-righteous/ judgmental/ and angry and don't see with the eyes of God. Humble people are going to be compassionate towards others no matter how sinful others have become. They know that they stand but for the grace of God. They truly want the best for those who have yet to repent. And so, they will mourn, weep, and pray with tears that God will save those who don't see as they should.

When one sins one might also get angry with one self. If the anger is too intense it comes from pride because we think we are better than what we thought or acted out. Such anger can and does often lead to self-hatred when used in attempting to create change interiorly. And when we hate in a context, then we can't love in the same context. This needs to be

---

[26] Matthew 5:4

avoided. Perfectionists are usually hard on and get angry with themselves (and therefore do it to others too). God is not petty or quick to anger. God is slow to anger. We need to see ourselves the way God sees us. When we mourn, and cry out to God with repentant hearts. A repentant heart is not an angry heart but a contrite heart. God wants us holy and righteous more than we want it. If one finds one is angry with oneself, one needs to accept it but not stuff it, and to refuse to hurt/ motivate/ or manipulate others and oneself with it. There is help[27] on how to healthily navigate this very unhealthy strategy or tendency.

There are two kinds of angers. The first comes from experiencing injustices and is more like a signal, the other is chosen as a tool to pressure changes such as supposed personal repentance, or in the things people do that we dislike. The first anger is healthy, and the last anger is unhealthy.

When anger is like a signal that goes off in us then it is telling us something is wrong interiorly or exteriorly. This anger is meant to get us to act and make things right and is very healthy. The key is to not try to wrestle such anger away. Rather it is a call meant to marshal us to act in kind, caring, and warm ways so the stuff that is wrong gets dealt with in healthy ways. This anger is not a moral fault, if we believe this anger is a moral problem then we will get angry with our anger and that just makes us more twisted, confused, and

---

[27] Cf. Rene Lafaut, *Dismantling the Tree of Knowledge of Good and Evil Within So Love Can Thrive*

useless in the face of injustices, and it impedes our ability to meekly question our expectations of people or ourselves that may have triggered our anger.

Yet, Another Beatitude Explained:

For a long time, I only saw "mercy" as something dispensed by a judge towards a lawbreaker ((i.e.) to forgive a debt, a moral wrong, or a criminal act). But now I see it as having a much wider range of meaning. I see it as compassionate or kindly forbearance shown not only toward an offender, or an enemy, but towards another person in one's power to help (such as those who are less fortunate or poor, or in need of clothing, healing, food, and love ((i.e.) human warmth)). To be merciful means to be compassionate, have pity, or show benevolence. Mercy sets people free: from prisons, burdens, debt, guilt, meanness, hatred, anger, and petty attitudes, but also brings healing to hurts, injuries, and diseases (spiritual, social or biological).

Jesus said in the Gospel of Matthew: "Blessed are the merciful, for they shall receive mercy."[28] One can't earn mercy, so the only reason merciful people receive mercy is because they are the only ones who understand it, and desire it because they do to others what they want others to do to them. In Matthew 25, Jesus describes the Final Judgment: those who were merciful, receive mercy; those who were proud and only out for themselves, or cared only about their own image, and treasured money or wealth more than the

---

[28] Matthew 5:7

human in need that crossed their paths, found themselves in such a position where they could not receive God's forgiveness (God cannot force His forgiveness on them) and so they experienced God's presence in such a fearful, untrusting, judgmental, jaded, and disagreeable way even though God is not that way at all.

But receiving mercy is not left only for the final judgment. Those who dispense mercy now, will often receive mercy in this life too. For instance, when we forgive someone who wronged us, God forgives us. Also, I know that there have been times when I have acted mercifully (helping others in need) and in response God has totally granted me mercy with me not deserving any of it which is how mercy is defined. What I'm trying to say is that when we are positive towards people we draw positivity to ourselves, just like people who are negative draw negativity towards themselves.

Just because God in the end will have mercy on those who are merciful does not mean that we ought only be merciful to those who are merciful today. Chances are we may know nothing about the history or character of those who cross our paths. We can't probe or question people to decide whether they are merciful before we are merciful to them. They might never have felt love, have gone through very difficult and dark experiences, been rejected, hurt, hated, shamed, or abused. Such people may be very hungry for love and mercy. Should we deny them that? No! You can't give what you have never received. Those who are callus and hurt others can be viewed as enemies, but we are called to love and be merciful to our enemies just like God is merciful to all of us. The healthiest way to kill an enemy is to make them your friend.

7 USING NON-VIOLENCE AS A PATHWAY TO PEACE

I am slowly getting to understand an area that has stymied me my whole life, and I am learning to not attack/ tackle situations or things blindly. What occurs in red-text below is the wisdom I got from a speech Derek Flood gave online. It has shed light on a huge area of discomfort and unease that required healing in my heart (Thank you, Derek for permission to share it):

It is so true that following blindly a set of instructions gets people hurt. [The only acceptable blind-love is romantic-love.] Unquestioningly being obedient to anyone especially confusing Scriptures leads to abuse. We cannot be faithful and honest if we don't know how.[29]

Jesus is the Light of the world. His truth sets us free. When we follow Him we walk in the light meaning we are led to see and aren't blind in the areas we are following Him in. Spiritual blindness is looked upon as an illness not a strength in the NT. And even when we follow Jesus, we are asked to renew our minds. Meaning that we have blind spots that He wants to heal and instead to bring us understanding in such dark places in our lives. Patiently waiting (searching for) on Him through an interactive relationship is key to uncovering blind spots and gaining freedom to love people more deeply.

Enemy love means to love our enemies no matter what they

---

[29] Video feed from Derek Flood

throw at us.

Rome's cross had to do with coming down on those convicted to death like a hammer in a bloody, hateful, ridiculing, forceful, retributive, crushing, and shameful way; whereas God in Christ on the cross was love in the midst of and in spite of the violence and He intended to expose to the world and us the insanity of crucifixion. Crucifixion is a grave injustice just like the NT says.[30]

When we pierced Jesus, in response He released water and blood both of which are symbolic of life not poison/ hatred/ malice/ judgment. Jesus came to give life, and that to the full. The New Testament (NT) teaches that in the past (i.e. OT) God was partially and imperfectly revealed, but that in Jesus we have the full revelation of God's character, nature, motives, and desires. God the Father did not come down like a hammer on Jesus during His Passion: indeed, the NT says God was in Christ on the cross reconciling the world to Himself. The cross and all Rome poured into it was not a healthy thing. Jesus came to expose it for what it was. Jesus' actions on the cross were pure, passionate, caring, peaceful, wise, and hit the mark on where our maladies as the human race are.

Jesus did not come to glorify the cross! He came to undo the works of the devil. He came to love and share His life with us. He joined in solidarity the despised, the unwanted and rejected; He sided with us, shared our weaknesses, and

---

[30] Video feed from Derek Flood

therefore the world powers wanted Him to pay for His loyalties, to hurt Him, and to somehow kill His popularity; they wanted to stop Him from reconciling the world to God, but it backfired and Jesus won the world and those who believe in Him. Even though our flesh crucified and rejected Jesus on the cross; Jesus did not reject us on the cross! What love He showed to us in this: the creator, despised and hated by His creation; yet the creator forgives creation and with outstretched - arms embraces us and so wins us by becoming weak by taking the hard way.

Love of enemies is not simply a refusal to engage in violence. Rather it is a better and more effective way of resolving conflict and ending hurt. It is not unrealistic or illogical. Nor is it opposed to a healthy desire to protect our loved ones and ourselves.

Retributive justice means being hard on those who are our enemies and to come down like a hammer on them because the thinking is: if we don't punish evildoers, then crime will run rampant. Retributive justice is violent payback to enemies and criminals.[31]

In many Christian circles the crucifixion of Jesus is seen as God's retributive justice through what is called penal substitution (i.e. god's justice meant that he had to punish us. But he wanted to forgive us so Jesus apparently took our punishment on himself and in doing so god vented his wrath on Jesus to supposedly enabling him to forgive and love us). I

---

[31] Video feed from Derek Flood

held to this view for a long time, but it is skew (riddled with problems) and devoid of enabling us to go to the center of love's source or understand God's love. Can someone buy your love? If so, is it still love? No, it isn't! Neither can anyone buy God the Father's love, because if they do it isn't love anymore. Therefore, Jesus did not buy God's love for us on the cross! It miss-represents who God is and casts him in the "molds of some demon gods" who in OT times demanded from certain communities that their infants be sacrificed through fires in order to find peace, prosperity, blessing, and a supposed hope. These communities were held in fear of the future by the demon-gods they worshipped.

But...

What if justice is about mending and healing and not coming down hard on transgressors? [32]

When I realized this, an old memory came to mind; I was a schoolboy in South Africa and my playmates were scrapping in the playground. I was trying to make peace among them so that they wouldn't get into trouble, but the school principal came over to see what was happening and, misjudging the situation perhaps because I was the biggest kid, blamed me and hit me.
Lord God, I forgive the principal for his action and I repent in faith from my reaction towards him which was wanting him to feel the pain he put me through: I wanted revenge.
Restorative justice is the framework for enemy love...

Love of enemies is a general principle applicable to both

---

[32] Video feed from Derek Flood

individuals and society which has many context-specific applications

Turning the other cheek (fighting oppression, exposing injustices of oppressive regimes (Gandhi and Martin Luther King are good examples of this)) is one particular application of the larger principle of enemy love. Turning the other cheek is not always effective or appropriate.[33]

It is wise to turn the other cheek when it comes to speech and communicating with people when things don't go our way or situations anger us (responding with kindness instead of insult for insult is turning the other cheek verbally). Our tongues can be weapons. Choosing to bless whomever we talk with will go a long way to stopping verbal and physical violence. Turning the other cheek when it comes to speech ought to be universal because if we can't be peaceful while talking we may escalate to violence actions.

The assumption is that force or violence will get things done... fact is this is wrong: Non-violent campaigns are more than twice as effective at resolving conflict than violent campaigns.[34]

The above has to do with bringing healing to those who transgress rules embraced by those cultures where the wrongs are done. But the ideas lend themselves to the theme of not using "might" to get one's way in ordinary situations in everyday life. I know that the principles apply to me, because

---

[33] Video feed from Derek Flood
[34] Video feed from Derek Flood

there has been a hard/ cold/ damn-it I got to force it mentality in me to get my way for a long time.

So, in the past when it came to me loving my family members, the dog, all the people at work and in the world I wanted to come down with force (which came from a hard place in my heart) on everyone to get what I saw as reasonable or just plainly my own way. I knew that this was wrong and I tried to suppress it, and stifle it but it worked often enough for me to have some confidence in it. After all something deep in my heart resonated with this darkness, but now I know it's roots: it was because I believed the lie that "might" was better than weakness or "kindness". Thank you, Lord Jesus, Father God, and Holy Spirit for showing me the errors of my ways and giving me liberating truths that are slowly transforming my actions into love, light, and kindness in a more compassionate way! Amen and Amen!

When we focus purely on what we want using war (think anger, meanness, force and threats), then we usually don't care about what our enemy/ neighbor wants. We have become selfish. Realizing that we don't have to go to war and that there are more effective ways to bring peace is where it is at. When we realize and embrace this: non-violence as the better way to peace then we begin to care about our enemy/ neighbor and their energy will begin to change for the better too if not already. Unselfish peace becomes ours.

We can be tempted to harden our hearts when our neighbor/ enemy wants to go in what looks like the opposite direction to our goal. When we choose to stomach this at least temporarily we begin to find out slowly that we don't have to be selfish because the detour is also on our way to the goal. When we show kindness to our neighbor/ enemy they will recognize it and they will very likely be determined to show us kindness in return and so help us come to our goal too.

Strangely enough when I first got ill with schizophrenia and attended a church service somebody recited out loud the following verse:

> 'Not by might nor by power, but by my Spirit,' says the LORD Almighty.[35]

I remember believing it but not understanding it fully. I knew at the time that it meant I needed the Spirit to get through my trial, and that acting independently would secure my spiritual death certificate. But now I see that there are wider ramifications: Only by God's Spirit can I love supernaturally, and also come from a gentle kind and loving place when interacting in all my relationships.

Note: When I seek to use violence on my enemy when my enemy seeks it on me, then I become like my enemy. This knowledge is what I've aimed for. Having correct theology does not mean healthy relating. Spiritual illnesses need to be healed. To be no longer tempted to use force or violence inappropriately is my goal. There is a methodology to help[36] achieve this.

---

[35] Zechariah 4:6

[36] Cf. Rene Lafaut, *Dismantling the Tree of Knowledge of Good and Evil Within So Love Can Thrive*

I now realize that when Jesus went to the cross and was raised up He drew all peoples to himself, and they brought that which was not submitted to God with them; namely their independent wills, broken intellects, and warring emotions, desires and attitudes. Jesus did this so that we could see that our independence or flesh wanted to crucify Him. And with the Holy Spirit's gentle nudging we are cut to the heart as we see our sins nail Jesus to the cross and so we are healed. Those whose eyes are opened to this daily, carry their own crosses and in so doing don't live solely for earthly pleasures, but for supernatural love through being led by the Spirit through relationship.

Following the way of "enemy love" does not start with a high ideal or my own goodness. Rather its motivation and source of strength is the person of Jesus together with His example of enduring the cross and His rationale for doing so. A philosophy by itself does not give the power needed to carry it out no matter how good the philosophy is.

8 HYPOCRISY AND LEGALISM

Who hasn't had standards, and naively thought that they kept them? When we think we keep them all then the trouble starts. Who hasn't had high standards one moment, and the next moment broken them without being aware of it until later, usually because it is pointed out to oneself by another person? When we are hypocritical and don't know it we are to be pitied above all people. Getting to the point where we know that we have hypocrisy is crucial for real change.

Whatever way a person shows hypocrisy, if they never repent from it, then they will do a lot of harm to others and themselves in those contexts. People who have hypocrisy and don't know it have become blind to some or all the light that has been granted to them. Their consciences are not working as they should. Their hearts have become callused. They have pride because they see themselves as better off than they really are.

A hypocrite is one who says to others: "Do such and such..." but would never do it himself or herself. A hypocrite is one who would say: "Don't do such and such..." but does it him or herself in total abandon.

Those who see their sins and hypocrisy for what they are know that they need mercy, and are more likely to dispense that mercy to others. Jesus said, "Blessed are the merciful, for they will be shown mercy".[37]

---

[37] Matthew 5:7

Jesus the humblest man who ever walked on the face of the earth once said:

> Yet a time is coming and has now come when the true worshippers will worship the Father in spirit and truth, for they are the kind of worshippers the Father seeks. God is spirit, and his worshippers must worship in spirit and in truth.[38]

In the past, I would always struggle to understand these words, but now I think that I do. When Jesus says, we will worship God in spirit, He means that we will worship according to the real meaning and intent of His words. When Jesus says that we will worship in truth, He means that we will worship God with diminishing amounts of hypocrisy as we journey with Him and persevere.

There is a vast difference in worshipping according to the letter of Jesus' word, as opposed to the spirit. When we worship according to the letter we are doing as the Pharisees do – we make the outside of the cup clean but the inside of the cup is still filthy. It's our motives, energy, and methodology that God cares about. "For it is from within, out of a person's heart, that evil thoughts come, sexual immorality, theft, murder, adultery, greed, malice, deceit, lewdness, envy, slander, arrogance and folly."[39] Who isn't convicted by this list? Humility moves from practicing darkness to practicing what the Light teaches. Jesus is the Light. Light is a metaphor for goodness, love, and tolerance.

---

[38] John 4:23-24 (emphasis mine)
[39] Mark 7:21-22

Christians practice light only when they abide in the Light: Jesus.

The Christian walk is about faith working itself out in love. This involves in some sense keeping the commands of the Son of God through caring, grace and truth.

If we keep all the credit for ourselves by keeping the commandments to love, then we are self-righteous, and that is worse than hypocrisy.

Legalism (A false Humility):

To be legalistic means that one is not keeping a law for what it was intended. Put another way, legalism occurs when we don't understand the real intent of a command handed down to us from God and invent rules to keep it yet miss the real intent of that command. These rules often fall in line with the letter or wording of the command, but they oppose the spirit (real intent) of the command. Legalism also occurs when we make certain commands too absolute and don't make room for the exceptions. Rules often are intended to remove abuses, but when we forget what those abuses are, then we land up applying the rules where they were never intended to reach.

Legalism is using what is holy in a wrong manner. Legalism involves being spiritually impaired or blind.

Legalism is using truth with the wrong focus, wrong energy, and wrong motives; it seeks sacrifice instead of mercy.

Legalism is into conformity, not transformation.

Legalistic people may tend to see themselves as the good

guys and those who oppose them in some way as the bad guys.

Legalistic people may be quick to judge, and forget that they are just as guilty of sin as those they are condemning.

Legalistic people may be quick to pick up stones and throw them, when God weeps tears of Living Water or love: who is known as the Holy Spirit.

Legalistic people are likely to be all for retributive justice (is there such a thing? I think revenge is a better word).

Legalistic people may use God's commandments to harshly, coldly, and meanly condemn people for not keeping them. They forget that they too don't keep all of those same commands.

Legalistic people see life through a distorted lens called judgmentalism.

The Law was intended to show us what love is, along with what sin is. But many people wrongly use it to try to "supposedly" get right with God. No one can get right with God by keeping the law. Getting right with God has to do with accepting His grace and mercy through faith in Jesus. The Law makes nothing right or perfect.

Legalistic people will tend to focus on minor issues to the exclusion of weightier matters and see it as practicing humility.

For example, legalistic Christians may focus on not being involved with tobacco, alcohol, dancing, bowling alleys, movies, glamour magazines, cards or gambling, expensive clothing, certain music, or watching TV. They may also see carrying a Bible to church as an expression of righteousness.

Legalistic people may also view refusing to swear, or stuffing anger as rooted in humility. Showing indignation for blatant violations of certain visible standards alone might appear as righteous behavior to legalistic people.

What do the following words mean: "The letter kills, but the Spirit gives life"[40]? To paraphrase it I think "it means that keeping the outward appearance of the Ten Commandments can't give life by itself. Jesus is the source of life."

Thinking that theological accuracy implies one is also automatically practicing it, is also a form of legalism or loss of reality. When this happens, one is not in touch with where one is at practically and morally speaking. One has become blind to what the Light says and will have a higher opinion about one self than is warranted.

Inventing rules that agree with our vague and wrong or misguided understanding of what God seems to expect, is also legalism. When we think that God dislikes celebrations, or wants us to continually feel guilty and be conscious about His supposed anger, then we are legalistic. It is a good thing to celebrate the birth of a new year, the birth of a new romance, and, also of all new life coming into the world. Some people groups have never celebrated the gift of new life because nowhere in the Bible do they see Jesus commanding us to celebrate His own birthday. They forget

---

[40] 2 Corinthians 3:6

that Jesus would only command us to celebrate His birthday if He were proud. As His followers, we are free to celebrate every facet of His existence – including His birth. Jesus said that the Holy Spirit would bring Him Glory.[41] Jesus never said, "Don't celebrate My birthday."

When we obey rules in ways that miss the real intent, then we are becoming legalistic. This is why counsels, and governments everywhere are continually rewriting laws because they get dated and no longer protect what they were intended for because people invent loopholes.

When Jesus said that the Pharisees, "strain out a gnat but swallow a camel."[42] He was saying that they were majoring on minor issues, and minoring on major concerns – and this is what legalistic people do. Legalistic people have abandoned in some ways the path to truth and authentic love. The search for and living out of the Truth that is motivated by caring is part of what it means to be humble. We all have some legalism in our lives.

A cure to legalism is to view holiness as spiritual healthiness. This means that we slowly abandon blind spots, get understanding that is based on caring for people knowing love does no harm to one's neighbors.

There are two extremes: (1) Seeking to obey God's commandments and (2) following the Maxim: "Love does no harm."[43] Those who only focus on the commandments

---

[41] Cf. John 16:14
[42] Matthew 23:24
[43] Romans 13:10

become legalistic; whereas those who only focus on; "love does no harm" become humanistic. We need to be somewhere in the middle. Legalism empties God's commands of meaning. But if we ignore God's commands then we will miss much of what God sees in our hearts. We need to hear God speak if we are to truly love. God speaks to everyone. Many tune His voice out, and listen to the world, the pleasures of the flesh, and the devil instead.

Ultimate Legalism:

The ultimate form of legalism is when we keep the commandments of God outwardly but independently of God which means it is done self-righteously. Such devotion is devoid of the real intent and source of God's commandments.

The Importance of Humility:

The first beatitude, "Blessed are the poor in spirit for theirs is the kingdom of heaven"[44] is a promise. Whether you are a newly baptized Christian, or been one most of your life, it doesn't matter – being "poor in spirit" is what keeps you saved. Even if you go through blistering trials like I did, it is still necessary during the trial, and afterwards. So, what does it mean to be "poor in spirit"? I offer the following definition: To be "poor in spirit" means to see ourselves in need of the Spirit. It means to have some humility and to be growing in it. It means to be aware of our riches but not proud because of them. It means to be aware of our poverty but not envious of

---

[44] Matthew 5:3

65

others because of their riches. Humility in an area means we are teachable in that area. We are proud or puffed-up when we look down on others.

9 ENVY

Envy can be hard to detect or even disagree with when it springs up out of the soil of our hearts. I've found myself saying many times when I beheld my poverty, and another's riches, "It's not fair – God gave it to them so why not to me also?" We hear many people say this from time to time, but it goes against humility. What God has done for others, He won't always do for you, or me. And it seems so unfair to us. If we set our hearts on what others have, we covet, and break one of the Ten Commandments. Coveting hardens our hearts towards those who have what we want because we say to ourselves that we must have what they have – "it's only fair."

It is not necessarily wrong to want something that our neighbor has, if it is available. But if we want the actual thing our neighbor has and set our hearts on it, if they can't or won't give it to us, then we may very well become unloving towards them. This un-loving attitude may show itself in anger, hostility, aggressiveness, rage, hatred, impatience, jealousy, self-pity and unhealthy actions or movement meant to attain what we covet. And God ultimately gets blamed if He doesn't come through for us because of envy. For those who already don't believe in God, it becomes another reason to hate the possibility of His existence. If the good we desire can't be gotten (such as intelligence, understanding, power, musicality, ect.) we might harden our hearts towards God, or become obsessively jealous of those who do have what we want.

If we believe in the existence of God, our prayers may become demands for Him to show His fairness, and His loyalty to our causes. We may dress up our envy by trying to entice God with the idea that we could do a lot of good with His gifts. But ultimately, we want it for ourselves. And so, we lose our thankfulness when God gives us the cold shoulder. Or, we persevere in prayer thinking that God might still reward us. If we do persevere in prayer, and envy is motivating our prayer, then our hearts will get colder and colder. But still we might persist with our cleverly concealed demands. After all, we quote the Bible when it says:

> Delight yourself in the LORD and he will give you the desires of your heart.[45]

We can't delight in God when we are envious of others. We can't delight in money and God at the same time. We will either hate one or despise the other. God knows our hearts.

The Bible speaks a lot about the dangers of putting money first. But people can forget this when they hear Jesus saying, "ask and you will receive".[46] Such shortsightedness is crippling.

Delighting oneself in the Lord is more than having enthusiasm for Him, or more to the point – having enthusiasm for what He can do for one. The Bible says that humanity doesn't live on bread alone, but on every single word that comes from the mouth of God.[47] This is a difficult statement, that Bible

---

[45] Psalm 37:4
[46] John 16:24
[47] Cf. Matthew 4:4

believers complacently quote at one time or another. But we can forget that there is much teaching in the Bible that is hard to chew on and digest, let alone make a part of our lives. Re-read the Sermon on the Mount in the Gospel of Matthew some time.[48]

If we delight in the LORD (not our understanding of Him, or what He can do for us), then He will give us Himself in whom we delight. Can He give us anything greater?

The whole practice of delighting in the LORD has to do with taking up one's cross daily and following Jesus. The Gospel cannot be compared to a comfortable couch that we sit in while being entertained by the miracle worker Jesus for the rest of our earthly lives. For Jesus, it was a rugged wooden beam that weighed Him down and that He needed help carrying. Psalm 1 begins with:

> Blessed is the one who does not walk in step with the wicked or stand in the way sinners take or sit in the company of mockers.

Notice the progression above: Walking, standing, and finally sitting, i.e.) moving from action to inactivity and eventually poisoning other people's minds with one's speech.

I have thought that my insights were noble and constructive when in fact I only wanted my own way. Love does not seek its own way (it isn't selfish or demanding or meanly expectant). Here is my interpretation regarding the dispute

---

[48] Cf. Matthew 5:1-7:29, or Luke 6:20-6:49

between Mary and Martha:[49]

Martha indulging in self-pity, complaining, and in anger asked for judgment and a 'supposed' justice from Jesus trying to make her sister Mary help her. That was the worst part. Mary choose the better part. Mary chose joy and that in the presence of Jesus! Mary chose joy; Martha chose self-pity/ complaining/ judging/ anger. That is why Jesus said Mary chose the better part. Everyone knows that good works are important, and, also that learning is important. It wasn't about "work vs. visiting/ learning" both are important. It was about "self-pity/ judging/ anger vs. joy".

Jesus taught in the Sermon on the Mount for us to not judge or condemn people. One judges and condemns when one doesn't look in the mirror and makes sober observations with the light given. Self-pity, complaining, judging, and anger all go together. When they are together often they are an unhealthy mix, and in such cases, they spring from pride. Mary chose the better part; Jesus said it would not be taken from her. Martha chose the worst part, but Jesus wanted to take it from her if she would allow it. He eventually did!

Look at God's attitude. He doesn't have a critical spirit towards his children. By critical spirit I mean one where He is constantly looking for flaws and mistakes to rub into our faces or to attack us with. We should have the attitude that says, "There go I but for the grace of God." Also, if an unbeliever is not asking for our correction then likely we should not give it

---

[49] Cf. Luke 10:38-42

to him or her, unless of course, the person is in real danger of gravely hurting or harming someone else. But it needs to be done as gently as possible, without making a big scene out of it, non-judgmentally, and without preaching. Also, spare the other person's pride or dignity by not pointing out his or her fault in front of a crowd. Do it privately.

I was corrected many years ago by a friend after I road my bike in a irresponsible and reckless fashion almost hurting a lady. I could have badly injured her because of my lack of care and disrespect. Right after the incident, my friend who witnessed the incident assertively pointed out to me that I needed to ride my bike with more care and respect so that those around me would not get hurt. I felt hurt by what he said at first, but humble enough to listen to what he said and act accordingly.

I felt hurt for years by his rebuke because my pride was wounded (I had conceit). Then years later I attempted to correct a different person in a gentle fashion only to hurt him or her by ending the correction with a preachy and judgmental tone. By being preachy and judgmental I hurt my second friend's pride. As these memories met within my mind I realized I needed to heal the past and make further amends to the person I was preachy and judgmental towards.

I have no power to change anyone else except myself, and even that can be a formidable challenge. The opening line in the Serenity Prayer admits we have limitations when it comes to ourselves and more so with others.

In the past, I used to think that it was okay to be

constructively critical towards one's spouse/ fiancée/ girlfriend/ or boyfriend until I read the book called *Becoming A Family That Heals*[50]. Now I know that when one is judged one will be made to feel guilt or inferiority and one will likely get angry and defensive as a result and start to argue and point out the dirty laundry of the one doing the criticizing. So, I have been taught that instead of being critical I need to use an "I" statement. That way they don't feel judged by me; get defensive, and feel angry and therefore judge me back. Being critical or judgmental might feel powerful, righteous or noble at first but a power struggle usually results from such attempts to change one another.

---

[50] Drs. Beverly and Tom Rodgers, *Becoming A Family That Heals*, Tyndale House Publishers, copyright 2009, Chapter 13.

10 BEARING GOOD FRUIT AND BAD FRUIT?

Many Christians are deceived into thinking that they don't have any good behavioral fruit. When it comes to righteousness they see themselves in a pictorial way as wearing dung-covered clothing. By wholesome fruit the Bible means: "love, joy, peace, patience, kindness, goodness, faithfulness, gentleness and self-control."[51] I agree that wearing dung-covered clothing is the way we all start out, but in 1 John 1:9 it says:

> If we confess our sins, [God]... is faithful and just and will forgive us our sins and purify us from all unrighteousness.

This purification is a process that we cooperate with God in bringing about. Some people think that we must change our behavior and then confess our sins for God to forgive us. This is wrong. When we confess our sins, we are acknowledging them as wrong, and we wouldn't do it unless we wanted to change. We may want to change and not have a clue as how to go about it. 1 John 1:9 says that after confession God starts the process of cleansing. The cleansing process further involves repenting in faith and renewing the mind in co-operation with God and becoming dependent on His constant grace. There are helpful[52] strategies to implement this.

When we have a compulsion towards something, then we are

---

[51] Galatians 5:22
[52] Cf. Rene Lafaut, *Dismantling the Tree of Knowledge of Good and Evil Within So Love Can Thrive*

not free to defy the attraction or act, and so we are slaves to the compulsive sin. If we have a compulsion, and want to overcome it and don't know how, we shouldn't feel guilty about it. Attempting to do more and try harder won't work. Praying to Jesus and listening to what He asks us to do is the path to take.

We don't abide in Jesus by impressing God with our piety, good works, loyalty, holiness, wisdom, degrees, study habits, titles, pedigree, accomplishments and traditions.

We don't stay in the True Vine [or Jesus] by self-righteously earning God's favor through good works.

We love by staying in the Vine. We abide in the Vine when we embrace humility and stay teachable. By abiding in the Vine, we are connecting with the Vine: Jesus, and that means we are seeking His face; we are God-centered, not pleasure centered. This means we nurture communication with Jesus, and trust in Jesus, and we learn slowly to give ourselves freely to God, and to pursue Him so that we can follow Him. When we get to know Him through the rough times we will learn to celebrate Him, and not to be caught up in ourselves. We are not fully abiding in the Vine when we put angry pressure on people or ourselves; or when we go to a place of "life is so unfair" and coldly demand our way with self-pity.

God is not deliberately looking out for reasons to cut us out of the tree of life. He is looking for ways to get us closer to Himself. And when we are close to Him we will naturally do His will. His will for us is to love, and love springs from thankfulness and caring for people. Jesus is a Christian's foundation of thankfulness. This can be difficult to nurture when we go through periods that make us question where God is, why He lets things happen like evil triumphing over good.

No one can supernaturally love apart from God because God is love. Wherever God is, so is supernatural love. Wherever supernatural love is, so is God. When one loves supernaturally one will automatically give God His due. God is worthy of all our worship or devotion because He is love. God deserves our worship and gratitude. As far as the natural loves are concerned (i.e. those loves we are conceived with in our mothers' wombs); they are good as far as they go but they fall short of supernatural love or perfection. The natural loves are a preparation for the supernatural loves. God has given the natural loves to us, but some people have yet to figure out that the loves they have naturally come from God[53]. The supernatural loves complete, extend or lift the natural loves to where they ought to be.

Some sins are symptoms from seemingly unrelated past sins that I call virus sins. We may be able to control the symptoms for a while, if we are lucky. But we should take the right medication to get rid of the virus if we don't want the symptoms to keep flaring up repeatedly. They are called virus sins because they damage a person's spiritual health in more than one way. Holding a resentment is one such kind of sin. Resentments not only cause us to become more un loving, but they cause addictions. The addiction might seem

---

[53] I am in debt to a friend for this insight.

unrelated to the resentment, but they are linked.

Some sins are like bad fruits that we forcibly taste, but the bad fruit come with fruit flies, that carry lies, that can enter our hearts when we choose to unwisely receive and believe them. These fruit flies (or devils) carry lies that fertilize "the tree of knowledge of good and evil" within us that cause us in turn to bear bad fruit like judging, meanness, hostility, hatred, etc. that in turn cause us to become slaves to compulsive sins like judging, and meanness, besides other addictive behaviors.

We can try to pull the bad fruits off the tree within as much as we want to, but the bad fruit will keep growing back so long as that part of the tree lives. If we dismantle and pull the unwanted tree out of our hearts, and fully renew our minds and hearts, then we won't bear any of that fruit anymore, and then the branches in our eyes will be removed too. The eyes I am talking about are our consciences.

I have learned that sins such as addictions or compulsions are usually a harvest of bad fruit we reap; whereas the bitter root sins have to do with lies, resentments, vows, grudges, judgments, or un-forgiveness that come from wounds real or imagined that we perceive others to have committed against us. Jesus said, "For if you forgive other people when they sin against you, your heavenly Father also will forgive you".[54] With forgiveness comes healing.

Good Fruit from the Vine:

---

[54] Matthew 6:14

Many Christians say after bearing some good fruit that all the credit ought to go to God. This is not completely true. In John 15 for instance, Jesus views Himself as the true Vine, and us as the branches attached to Him:

I am the true vine,
and my Father is the vinedresser.
Every branch in me that bears no fruit
he cuts away,
and every branch that does bear fruit he prunes
to make it bear even more.
You are clean already,
by means of the word that I have spoken to you.
Remain in me, as I in you.
As a branch, cannot bear fruit all by itself,
unless it remains part of the vine,
neither can you unless you remain in me.
I am the vine,
you are the branches.
Whoever remains in me with me in him,
bears fruit in plenty;
for cut off from me you can do nothing.[55]

The branches that do bear good fruit do so for many reasons. The main reason is that they abide or remain in the true vine (i.e. they aim to practice humility; are teachable and follow Jesus through faith). We don't do good deeds to earn a place in the vine. We bear good fruit by staying in relationship with

---

[55] John 15:1-5, From The Jerusalem Bible © 1966 by Darton Longman & Todd Ltd and Doubleday and Company Ltd.

God by grace through humble faith in God. Having said this, the branches that do bear good fruit grow in this function because of the following reasons.

First the branches are pruned so that they will bear even more fruit. Being pruned means that the sucker branches are cut off. Sucker branches waste the precious sap that comes from the vine. Either pruning these branches from us mean we are disciplined painfully by God so that He can form character in our hearts through a faith that endures the suffering. Or it means that when we repent in response to Jesus' words we feel pain and withdrawal symptoms from those sins that we give up through His grace.

This is the meaning of the often-misunderstood words by Jesus that say:

> If your hand or your foot causes you to sin, cut it off and throw it away. It is better for you to enter life maimed or crippled than to have two hands or two feet and be thrown into eternal fire. And if your eye causes you to sin, gouge it out and throw it away. It is better for you to enter life with one eye than to have two eyes and be thrown into the fire of hell.[56]

The "hands" and "feet" that Jesus wants us to cut off are not our physical hands, or feet! They have to do with those dark desires, beliefs and attitudes of superiority that we agree with, that cause us to hurt people by our speech or behaviors, and that are so much a part of our lives that we are

---

[56] Matthew 18:8-9

committed to despite possibly our consciences' disapproval. We may get to the point where our consciences get too callused or seared in certain areas and so they no longer tell us right from wrong when it comes to our commitments to pride, our evil attitudes, and our dark desires because of our dark beliefs, and bad loyalties.

The reason Jesus calls these dark beliefs, desires and attitudes "hands" and "feet" is because to us they seem to be a natural part of the way we function. It's almost like we can't live without those parts in our day-to-day lives since they are compulsive, emotional, and entrenched. Thus, they cloud our perceptions of right and wrong and help us to embrace life-styles or habits that have developed over time that are immoral.

The "eyes" Jesus wants us to gouge out have to do with renewing our consciences or minds or the way we see or believe things. Either we will be ashamed of the fruit (and try to hide it), or we may embrace it thinking it is natural and become proud of it. Judging (hardening our hearts and getting angry with or judgmental towards) people who embrace and become proud of such dark-desired-lifestyles won't help. We are to love, tolerate, and respect every person. We are to hate sin (not in the emotional sense of the word) but in the sense of "not giving" ourselves to sin: to not glorifying the sin.

And it is amazing how we can justify these dark desires, beliefs, and attitudes, along with the dark schemes, and the dark fruit that they produce. Jesus knew just how glued to our lives they can become. For me, being a man, for the longest time I unnaturally, as far as God's design is concerned, thought that sexual lust outside of marriage was okay and healthy. There is help[57] to finding freedom and to give up such desires, imaginations and sins as these. Joining a healthy church community, or Christian based Twelve-Step groups can also help. Don't expect overnight success. Real change comes gradually, gradually, and then gradually through commitment and healthily searching with the light of Jesus.

We ought not feel guilty if we have bad desires or bad feelings yet resist them and where they can or do lead us to. Compulsions are dark desires that form addictions. Compulsions can have roots in un-forgiveness, judging, or hatred in our hearts or lies that we have swallowed, unhealed wounds inflicted by others, or resentments made in the past.

Either way, whether it is God disciplining us, or us feeling withdrawal symptoms through repentance, being pruned requires that we cooperate with the Vinedresser: God the Father.

Secondly, the living branches have precious sap flowing through them. This sap is the grace or power granted to us by the True Vine or Jesus. God wants to provide us with this grace, but we can block it through our pride, and judgments against other people. When we block the grace, we start to atrophy or die spiritually. We also need to continually ask for this grace or sap from God through prayer. Then, to believe

---

[57] Cf. Rene Lafaut, *Dismantling the Tree of Knowledge of Good and Evil Within So Love Can Thrive*

God is with us and that we are not alone by ourselves. This truth helps us to get connected to Jesus and it is a good idea to remind ourselves of this regularly.

This requires poverty of spirit on our part: the attitude that says, "Here go I but for the grace of God." Other Bible translations say God the Father is the "vine-grower" instead of "vinedresser". God wants us to grow in the fruit of His Spirit, but pride (hardness of heart, meanness, anger, displays of self-pity or judgmental-ism) blocks this growth. There is useful help[58] in renewing our minds and hearts.

When a person does not block the precious sap, practices humility, it means that they value people, honesty, and truth and refuse to use people for their own selfish gratification, i.e. They aren't lustful.

The fruit bearing branches are small compared to the Vine. We the branches should not compare our sizes to each other's because such pride leads to envy and jealousy. I hesitate to use the idea of "humans exercising muscles of love" because if there were such a thing then we would get proud quickly when we observe our hugeness compared to the littleness of others. God told me that He was digging tunnels of love in me a long time ago. That means that the supernatural love that flows out of me comes out of tunnels not muscles. These tunnels carry the Holy Spirit's empowering presence or grace through me and manifest as love. So, the bigger the branches the hollower we are, and

---

[58] Cf. Rene Lafaut, *Dismantling the Tree of Knowledge of Good and Evil Within So Love Can Thrive*

that means the more dependent we are on the Spirit (which means we have nothing to boast about). This dependence is an important reason on why we do abide in the true Vine: Jesus!

And fourth, the branches need to remain in the true vine to bear good fruit otherwise they die. God wants to lead us, but we need to follow Him if that's to be a reality. We need to be teachable. He wouldn't warn us to remain in the Vine if He didn't give us a choice in the matter. God cuts dead or unproductive branches out of the vine because they block grace or waste the precious sap.

Now it is true that if one wants to get to know and love somebody one must spend time with that person. Those whom we see spending very little Quiet Time with God in our opinion may be spending all the time God asks them to. We are not allowed to judge or condemn. We are all at different stages in our spiritual journeys. Some Christians might have some very black maladies within their hearts that keep them from prospering, growing, bearing much good fruit, and enjoying their walk with Jesus. Such healing may take years and years to deal with.

Patience is needed: not a whip, not judgmentalism, and not loading them with burdens of guilt such as: "if you'd only do what I do!" Also, it is really easy to get angry with someone who crosses our boundaries, to get all heated, and justified in our anger. And for resentments to take root. It may take time to work out what the roots are (commitments, beliefs or lies) to such dark reactions, and may take time for us to realize that we need to forgive and move on in love.

People are only responsible for the truth that they have heard or are aware of. God judges every single person by his or her own conscience, not by yours or mine. A Christian can only supernaturally love by abiding in the true Vine. Some non-Christians can love supernaturally too, and God gives them special graces to do it when they do it, even if they know nothing about abiding in the true vine: Jesus. The Bible says that those who love [supernaturally] are born of God. We should not fall into condemning or judging those who are not Christians as absolutely on their way to Hell. We need the attitude that says, "There go I but for the grace of God" when we see people out of control. This realization hinges on being aware of our dependence on God.

As we watch our branches supposed poverty or riches, and look at the neighboring branches' prosperity or poverty, one of the more difficult things to do is to fight off the envy and pride that so easily entangles us. This is because we often get heavenly riches confused with earthly riches. Our pride and envy can grow faster than the fruits of the Spirit. That's why we should do everything that the Vine, Sap, and Vinedresser require from us.

11 HOW DO YOU SEE YOURSELF?

What God has done for others, He won't always do for you, or me. That's one lesson. The opposite is also true. What God will sometimes do for you and me, He may not do for anyone else. If we lack an attitude of humility in this area, this becomes an opportunity for our pride to grow. Humility can't be faked in the heart. Following a bunch of rules outwardly will never produce humility. Pride can cause distance between us and God because we might think He favors us over others or others over us. This thinking is rooted in the idea that we are better than anyone else or deserving of what good anyone else has. Humility knows that we aren't better or worse than anyone else when it comes to sin. We are all sinners.

Some people might be more spiritually healthy than us, others less so. But we should not allow this to give rise to pride in our hearts. Others may start out in very unhealthy circumstances. But have made significant progress spiritually compared to us. While we may have started out in very healthy circumstances, but have squandered much. We shouldn't be measuring ourselves with others to feel good or superior. That is the kind of judging that Jesus forbids.

Pride leads to judging and coveting. Pride thinks it is the best, envy laments it isn't equal or better. You don't have to be rich to be proud. Even the poor can be envious, and therefore proud.

We all have some riches and some poverty. As far as our

poverty is concerned, we need to see ourselves as sinners in constant need of a Worthy Savior. Not just a savior from Hell, but a savior from sin. Even when we see ourselves as sinners, we don't have to constantly feel guilty about it, because one of our riches is the grace and forgiveness of a loving God and Father.

Some people believe if one views oneself as a sinner one will have low self-esteem. This is not necessarily true if one knows the love of the Creator, and believes that He values us despite our shortcomings and is rebuilding us.[59] Our self-esteem is not based on the shifting standards of a decaying society, but on the goodness of God.

The "rich" or "spiritually proud" may not be aware of their hunger and thirst for righteousness. They may be more concerned with what the world has to offer. They may be thankful for what they have, but have no one to thank except quite likely themselves or random chance. At the center of being "poor in spirit" or humble is "thanksgiving" to God. God can't command thankfulness from us, only through love is it possible for God to bring it about in us. If we are thankful to God for providing our needs and some of our wants, then we will pursue a relationship with Him, and we won't be susceptible to much self-pity. The more "light" we have, the more potential we have for realizing the companionship God offers.

God Is Good:

---

[59] Cf. Philippians 1:6

I initially said that God will sometimes not do for us as He has done for others, and that sometimes He will do for us what He won't do for others. Because of this, I don't want to leave the impression that God is capricious, or as fickle as some non-Christian voices assert. God is better than we can ever imagine. And so, I believe that He wisely desires to give or withhold things from us for our own good. When God gives a gift, He always does so with the purpose of blessing others through us. He gives so that we can give.

Because God gives to some and withholds from others, we are prone to jealousy. Sometimes when we see others wasting the gifts given them that we wrongly covet, we may be tempted to judge God as unwise in the giving and withholding of His gifts.

Having said this, I must say that God has His reasons for doing the things that He does. It may be to test us so He knows what we want. Even so, that doesn't mean that we will be consoled by His reasons, or that He is answerable to us when He acts. How can the clay say to potter, "Why have you made me this way?"[60] It is a statement of faith that God is Sovereign, Loving, Merciful, Gracious, and Just. When we are proud, we will judge God as being "empty-headed", thinking that we would do better than what He has done. When we are humble, we will work through the process of accepting our station in life one day at a time! We can have both attitudes at war within us when we have hardships and others have it easier than what we seemingly do. It isn't an all

[60] Cf. Romans 9:21

or nothing thing!

Learning to accept our lot in life is not always easy. When things are going according to plan, then being happy with whom we are is easy. However, if we feel our limitations when hardships occur (to us or others), then it is not so easy to be content. Whether the hardships are of our own making or someone else's, acceptance of our situations is a sign of our maturity. Honest and healthy acceptance requires eyes that are guided by faith. A faith that is rooted and grounded in Jesus Christ.

Acceptance of our shortcomings is the first of the Twelve Steps. Accepting our shortcomings doesn't mean that we don't want to make further progress in practicing the virtues. Rather when we admit that we are sinners, we do so because we don't want to continue in our evil ways. We are basically admitting or accepting that we are made for better things. God accepts us for whom we are, but loves us so much that He doesn't want to leave us as we are.

We are all somewhat spiritually blind. True, we only need a small glimpse of our falseness in the light of the truth to start the journey to wholeness. But if we don't want to be led into error we need to put our faith in the Truth: who is Jesus, because He won't lead us astray when it comes to growing in the freedom to love when we are open to it. Most religions hold to many truths, and all of them do contain varying degrees of error (none of us have it all together; and this includes Christianity). But I choose Christianity even though it manages to agree on 99% of revealed truth, but is divided on the remaining 1%. Christianity has Jesus and He is the anchor of my soul. Anyone who denies Jesus is not God's friend. However, God is the author of all the good and truth no matter where it is found; in any Religion. Yet, God is not the author of all that non-Christian Religions teach and that goes against solid Christian teachings. If He was, then He created contradictions, because most Religions have sharp disagreements on many doctrines with each other.

Becoming a Christian doesn't mean we should reject absolutely everything from the paths we have followed up until the point of conversion. There is genuine goodness and truth found in most world Religions.

Black and white (all or nothing) thinking or putting people, or Religions into boxes comes from or leads to judging, pride, anger, intolerance, and hatred: not love. I used to think that everything other than Christianity was counterfeit but now I know that there is genuine goodness and truth found in other Religions (and those people that adhere to those Religions) and that I need to respect this. I think that all the goodness and truth found in people from other religions as healthy guides to accepting the Gospel. This goodness and truth is given by God. We need to respect people of different faiths and pray that we don't get proud and arrogant and dismiss them as vehicles of meaning and truth. They are human, and we ought not to demonize them.

We need to respect people of different faiths and pray that we don't get proud and arrogant and dismiss them as vehicles of meaning and truth. They are human, and we ought not to demonize them.

If one looks at Religions as either real or fake currency, and believes that one's own faith is the real thing and every other Religion is fake currency. One will likely not be as loving, tolerant, and gentle towards those of other faith traditions. I know that was the case with me for a long time. One will be combative and suspicious instead of being a warm reconciler by building bridges on common ground. Love will evaporate when one has a combative stance. One will minimize the wrongs one's fellow believers have committed (past to present), and only look for and point out the dirty laundry belonging to everyone else's traditions as the supposed "evidence" of the fake-ness of the faiths they hold onto.

Very few people are argued into embracing a different faith tradition. Gentleness, respect, patience, non-judgmentalism, refusing to condemn, and loving others with their love language will always go farther than an angry and intolerant approach to evangelism. We can't demand that others put their trust in Jesus. Jesus always invites those He calls in a gentle kind non-judgmental fashion. So should we. We need to check and see what kind of energy we have in our hearts towards others in the contexts of what the New Testament teaches about Salvation through Jesus. If it is judgmental mean or angry or "us=righteous vs. them=evil" then we are not handling the truth in Scripture as God intended it to be used, and we need to repent. When people have objections to the Gospel we ought not become abrasive towards them. We should meet people where they are at and patiently explain the truths handed down to us in kindness, tears, gentleness and respect.

There are many humble people in religions other than Christianity. There are many proud people who claim to be Christians. I believe that many of those who are humble, and do belong to other faith groups, have been taught wrongly about who Jesus is and what He came to do; and have seen too much hypocrisy in some of His followers. It is hard to overcome such barriers. On the other hand, all Christians, myself included have inconsistencies in our doctrines, and the way that we see Jesus. We are also not perfect in love, compassion, and kindness towards others (who is?). If we were in these things, then we would have removed all the lies that keep us from being perfect in love, compassion, and kindness.

No sect, no denomination, and no following has the fullness of the truth. We all don't love like we ought to, and that means we are all believing lies of some sort that keep us from loving deeply and genuinely without hypocrisy, or we are ignorant of truths yet to be revealed. Truth sets free; the fullness of the truth would set us completely free in love. The book of Romans chapter twelve calls us to renew our minds. This is a continual process, and we are never done. Jesus is the fullness of the truth, not any one church denomination, not the Catechism, not the popes, and not the Bible; and when Jesus sets us free we will be free indeed. None of us know Jesus fully in this life, besides he is infinite. Jesus is the fullness of the truth, not any one church denomination.

We Christians often superimpose our beliefs onto what is written in the Bible and the Gospels, while some non-Christians read into their religious writings goodness and mercy. People who teach and consistently act out what it means to be merciful are living out the Gospel, whether or not they have heard the Good News proclaimed by Christians.

People who are merciful are that way because they see their own need for mercy. When they are offered God's mercy they eventually accept it.

God has no favorites. He loves each one of us more than we can possibly love ourselves or even imagine. He loves us because He made us.[61] And He made us so that He could love us. Before we did anything good or bad ourselves He loved us. Humble people will search and eventually find the God as seen in Jesus Christ. They will come to believe that all the good that they have experienced or will experience is God's gift to them. They also realize that good gifts can and often do come wrapped up in pain. People who open these gifts start the process of learning to grow in more humility/ love.

Proud people may likely not want anything to do with gifts that are wrapped up in pain. The humble will inherit what God offers[62].

Just Having a Fun Time Sinning; or Hungering and Thirsting for More?

When we who make up the Church look and see the

---

[61] I'm in debt to my Dad for this insight.
[62] Cf. the Beatitudes in Matthew chapter 5

behaviors of those outside the visible church, we can either be sympathetic, judgmental, or compassionate. The sympathetic will see those outside the church as having fun. The judgmental will see them as only sinners, and the compassionate will see them as thirsty people who don't know the counterfeit from the genuine life-giving Spirit freely offered. Both proud and humble people may see outsiders as sinning (but one condescendingly and the other with grief). Only the humble will see outsiders as thirsty for life.

The humblest man who ever walked on earth: Jesus, came to serve and not to be served. His humility meant giving of Himself through acts of love, instilling hope, and granting us a future.

It ultimately cost Him His life. He did not set earthly security as His top priority, but He trusted His Father. He even had no place to lay His head.[63] Out of love He took on our hardships, our suffering, and our presence to show His solidarity with us. Jesus who, "being in very nature God, did not consider equality with God [as] something to be grasped,"[64] but showed His active humility and love for us by sharing in our hardships and poverty.

Some people have the idea that humility is going up the social and economic ladders because they think that they deserve those things. That is how they view themselves.

Jesus' idea of humility meant going down those ladders. He

---

[63] Cf. Matthew 8:20
[64] Philippians 2:6

didn't seek out the crowds to bring glory to Himself; He sought out people so He could serve their best interests. This is seen in the Gospels, when He would command those that He healed not to spread the word about Him in certain regions of Judea.[65] He did this because He didn't necessarily want all the attention on Himself. His focus was to seek out the lost, those who felt guilty, the unloved, and those suffering from diseases. Large crowds made that sort of work difficult.

Jesus wanted to work one-to-one and in small groups as opposed to larger groups. Jesus would often walk many miles to do one good deed for just one person. He left the well fed to be near the hungry, the ill, and the downtrodden. He came to bring the Good News of God's mercy and grace to us who are far away. He came to bring mercy to those who had gone astray. But many reject Him.

Some so-called Christian evangelists would not be caught alive investing a lot of time, effort or money in a few people where, if their hearts were cleaner, their efforts would be better spent. This is because they have unholy ambition in their hearts. They want us to send them money regularly and use all kinds of manipulative techniques to do this. Their hearts seek fame, fortune, and ease, instead of God's will.

This does not mean that all evangelists are like that, or that it is necessarily wrong to seek large crowds to minister to. Humble people aren't pompous; they aren't full of self-

---

[65] Cf. Matthew 8:4, Mark 1:44, and Luke 5:14

importance. Humble people don't view themselves as the most important people around, and so don't have to be number one when it comes to being served or treated with respect. They consider others as more important than themselves out of humility and not deception.[66] They therefore become servants, not self-promoters.

Jesus was a keen observer of humanity. He could have been very critical of us and deservingly so. He managed to walk a fine line in-between continuously pointing out our wrongs and not seemingly showing approval of our sins. He is always gentle and meek. If He would have continually pointed out His disciples sins, they would have given up quickly because Jesus would have come across as a negative, nit-picker, judgmental, anal, pain in the butt. Jesus was full of grace.

[66] Cf. Philippians 2:3

12 GRACE OR PRIDE?

When I was a child, I was expected to do chores around the house like most children my age. But because of my immaturity, I got so angry with my brother who seemed to get away with doing almost nothing. As I watched my productivity, and his meager efforts I used to have fits of rage, sulked, shed tears, felt a lot of self-pity, and was envious with how he got away with it. I would cry out loud to Dad to try to end what I saw as the unfair distribution of work. I'm sure that had someone told me the story about Martha and Mary in Luke 10, I would have completely sympathized with Martha. I wanted life to be fair, and just. I saw life as unfair. So, I had a lot of self-pity/ anger/ and judgments and hence no joy. I was robbed of my joy by my self-pity. Pride led to depression/ self-pity/ anger/ judgments. Humility would have led to joy. Jesus said He would not take Mary's joy from her. He wanted to give Martha (me) the same joy in exchange for her (my) anger/ self-pity/ judging/ and pride.

Self-pity stems from a sense of unfairness and can be used to appeal to the pity of others to demand that one's desires be met. When we feel unfairness or covet stuff we can try to use angry pressure on others to get our way. Both these uses of self-pity and anger to manipulate other people into getting what we want is very unhealthy. People who use anger to get things or who are constantly angry will very likely not feel much compassion or caring for other people. Even though I personally embraced pride and angry pressure blindly, compulsively, decisively, subconsciously, without having to think about it, basically by default. I also wanted restorative justice, I wanted grace, and I wanted fairness. Just because we have pride does not mean that we don't want grace and don't want to become humbler. We need to respect this, God does. Proud people can be in touch with their hunger and thirst for righteousness. I know I did before God started helping me deal with my massive pride.

Submission does not mean I give parents, spouses, bosses, and governments absolute power. It does mean that we submit to what they have a right to expect. It also means I ought to give to these people what they want with clean energy. It means to not meanly complain, be self-pitying, and full of bitterness in the face of hardships/ disagreements. It means to respect, honor, and not slander when I disagree with what they request. It means to not whine, criticize, argue in disrespectful ways. If I do submit in healthy ways, then I won't engage in negative poor me attitudes. Humility means I am gentle and kind in the face of difficult relationships.

Pointing at Others?

I know that there are many people who decline the invitation to follow Jesus because in their eyes, Christians are just hypocrites. Some of these may have been deeply wounded sexually by Priests or Pastors or supposed Pillars in local churches. What a barrier to overcome! On the other-hand on Judgment Day, when Jesus asks those who sought pleasure "alone" why they did not seek to do His will (or accept His invitations), some of these people will have the lame excuse that they didn't do God's good will because they only saw imperfections in those who claimed to be committed to God. These people were only willing to do God's will if others would do it without hypocrisy. They wanted fairness, and knew nothing about grace. When Jesus asks us, "Why didn't you follow the light and do what is right?" Can we really respond with, "'Joe Blow' didn't do it, so why should I have attempted to have lived mercifully, compassionately, and humbly?" This seems more like an excuse made up to justify one's selfishness and laziness than anything else.

Is Forgiveness a License to Repeat?

We can rationalize un-forgiveness by saying that if we forgive a person for what they did to us, then we give them a license to do it again. But nothing can be farther from the truth.

When we forgive a fault of another person, we are agreeing not to take revenge on them. We are admitting that under the right conditions we could do the same or even worse. If we are honest with ourselves, we will see that we also hurt others as well. No one is perfect. When we forgive someone, we are not saying that they should go uncorrected at all by the proper authorities. Forgiveness sets us free from the hardness in our hearts. It sets us free from being victims the rest of our lives. Forgiveness helps us live with what others have wrongly done to us. Either way we will live with what people do to us anyways. Forgiveness helps it to be a pleasant arrangement.

Since we ourselves want mercy from God because we too

aren't completely innocent, forgiveness asks God to remove eternal consequences from those who injured us, if it is at all possible.

When we forgive, we are saying that we will continue to love our neighbors despite what they have done to us, or continue to do to us. We may be able to correct the offender in some situations but we are to leave the correction to the right authorities.

If we are a parent and our child has done something wrong, after we forgive them, we need to correct them when they are young. Even King David after being forgiven by God was disciplined. By discipline I mean to correct the person respectfully, gently, with care, patiently, and with healthy energy, truth and kindness. Discipline does not mean taking out the whip, being harsh or being forceful. Change that is fear driven creates a slave mentality.

If we think that we don't need to forgive someone who has wronged us because they haven't changed, we are wrong. If one doesn't forgive them one will forever be a victim. When we forgive, we set ourselves free through the grace of God to love our enemies from our hearts. We forgive for our own health. The bridge that we burn we need to cross as well. Jesus forgave sinful people who had yet to mend their ways while He still hung from the cross during His passion. For further evidence that forgiving is what we are supposed to do even when the agents of our hurts don't change their ways, consider the following New Testament Scripture:

> [Love]... does not dishonor others, it is not self-

seeking, it is not easily angered, it keeps no record of wrongs. Love does not delight in evil but rejoices with the truth.[67]

We are to love our neighbors, especially when they wrong us. And these verses are directed to us when someone wrongs us. We can't brood over an injury if we keep no record of wrongs, if we are to love those who hurt us. If we do hold records of wrongs, then we need to confess this genuinely to God who offers to forgive us and cleanse us of all unrighteousness. Love is gentle.

---

[67] 1 Corinthians 13:5-6

13 GOD OR MONEY?

For a long time, I pondered the following saying from Jesus:

> Do not store up for yourself treasures on earth, where
> moth and rust destroy, and where thieves break in and
> steal. But store up for yourselves treasures in Heaven,
> where moth and rust do not destroy, and where
> thieves do not break in and steal. For where your
> treasure is there your heart will be also.[68]

The key to interpreting and keeping this statement is in
recognizing the difference in the words "invest" and "store."
This isn't a command meant to make us aim at being dirt poor
as far as earthly wealth is concerned. It is however a
command meant to direct us to actively invest the wealth we
have been given for the good of others. If we have the gift of
being entrepreneurs, then this command is not meant to give
us a bad conscience. The minimum investment one can make
with one's monetary wealth is to invest it with a bank. If we
can do better, then we ought to try. Jesus is asking us in this
command to be bold, courageous, and wise in how we invest
our wealth and not to just play it safe.

Almsgiving is one way where we can invest our money to help
those suffering from disabilities, disease, hunger, thirst, or
hardships encountered from plagues, famines, war,
catastrophes, or poor economies. This kind of giving is always
necessary because there will always be those who can't

---

[68] Matthew 6:19-21

provide for themselves no matter what one does for them in the short term. If one has the gift of being an entrepreneur, then a second way to help the poor is to invest and create employment for those who can work and wouldn't have jobs otherwise. If we ourselves aren't entrepreneurs, then perhaps we should search for people who are, and give them chances of investing (through our help) in the lives of others.

Jesus is not against us multiplying our wealth. He is against us selfishly storing wealth for ourselves alone. He took a chance with investing in us (for our good), and He wants us to take the chance with investing in others (for their good). Jesus is asking us to wisely share what we have been given, and not to store in places where it can easily be lost. We are called to either share our wealth through almsgiving, or through creating jobs by investment. If a person can earn a wage to support her or his family, the person's self-esteem will skyrocket. To be dependent on others in a way that encourages laziness is just poor stewardship on the part of those who have wealth.

Now, "Jesus did tell the rich young man to give his money to the poor. But he didn't tell this to everybody. The young man loved and maybe worshiped money. It would have been good for his soul to give it away. But if someone has a spiritually healthier attitude, if someone sees money as a tool for helping others, then Jesus might not call him or her to give all his money away."[69] Another thing, Jesus often uses the literary device of hyperbole to shock and awaken us to what

---

[69] From my friend Alex

He expects from us. My guess is that He wants us to err on the side of generosity as opposed to stinginess when it comes to how we treat others with our money.

Fruits of The Spirit Versus Fruits from The Dark Side:

The idea of describing human acts, which might be either right or wrong as good or bad fruit, is very fitting. All natural fruits contain within them seeds whether they are bad or good tasting. We have all tasted both good fruit and bad fruit.

The seed in the good fruit is the message, the call to nobleness, the promise of life, and the invitation to relationship. When we taste good fruit we usually want more of it. Some eat the fruit and throw away the seed without planting it in or embracing it with their hearts. These people are like suckers on a vine that waste the precious sap. They will never grow any good fruit themselves so long as they keep doing this. Those who allow the seed from the good fruit to be planted and watered regularly in their hearts eventually become born of God.

> Dear friends, let us love one another, for love comes from God. Everyone who loves [supernaturally] has been born of God and knows God.[70]

When we eat bad fruits thanks to people hurting us somehow, we also have decisions to make. We can either throw the bad fruit along with its fruit flies away and embrace the way of forgiving, or we can receive the fruit flies to fertilize "the tree of knowledge of good and evil" within us

---

[70] 1 John 4:7

with unhealthy messages, lies, and invitations for revenge into our hearts to form anger, resentments, bitterness, and meanness. When we do the former we grow in spiritual health. When we do the latter, the "tree of knowledge of good and evil" gets further established in our lives along with the possibility of getting addicted to stuff or compulsively disrespecting and hurting others.

Love without truth is not love, but hypocrisy. Truth without love kills.

14 THE PARABLE OF THE TALENTS

In this section, I'd like to share an interpretation of a parable by Jesus recorded below. I came across the interpretation through my personal sufferings in life, and meditations:

> "Again, it will be like a man going on a journey, who called his servants and entrusted his property to them. To one he gave five talents of money, to another two talents, and to another one talent, each according to his ability. Then he went on his journey. The man who had received the five talents went at once and put his money to work and gained five more. So also, the one with the two talents gained two more. But the man who had received the one talent went off, dug a hole in the ground and hid his master's money.

> "After a long time the master of those servants returned and settled accounts with them. The man who had received the five talents brought the other five. 'Master,' he said, 'you entrusted me with five talents. See, I have gained five more.'

> "His master replied, 'Well done, good and faithful servant! You have been faithful with a few things; I will put you in charge of many things. Come and share your master's happiness!'

> "The man with the two talents also came. 'Master,' he said, 'you entrusted me with two talents; see, I have gained two more.'

"His master replied, 'Well done, good and faithful servant! You have been faithful with a few things; I will put you in charge of many things. Come and share your master's happiness!'

"Then the man who had received the one talent came. 'Master,' he said, 'I knew that you are a hard man, harvesting where you have not sown and gathering where you have not scattered seed. So I was afraid and went out and hid your talent in the ground. See, here is what belongs to you.'

"His master replied, 'You wicked, lazy servant! So you knew that I harvest where I have not sown and gather where I have not scattered seed? Well then, you should have put my money on deposit with the bankers, so that when I returned I would have received it back with interest.

"Take the talent from him and give it to the one who has the ten talents. For everyone who has will be given more, and he will have an abundance. Whoever does not have, even what he has will be taken from him. And throw that worthless servant outside, into the darkness, where there will be weeping and gnashing of teeth.'[71]

The parable always used to confuse me – what were the talents given in accordance with each servant's abilities? How did they invest these talents? And how did they get a return?

___

[71] Matthew 25:14-30

Yes, what are the talents?

For me, the parable eventually came to speak about what humble, and proud people do with the opportunities God provides each of us with. The parable of the talents speaks of the economy of salvation.

Once read, it becomes clear that the man going on a long journey is Jesus. And that Jesus entrusts His servants with talents. Servants are aware that they are commanded to accomplish certain tasks.

What then are the talents and ability mentioned in this parable? Clearly, the talents are given in accordance with our abilities.[72] So our talents and abilities can't be the same things. This is evidence that the talents spoken of here aren't aptitudes. If they were then the parable would be saying that we each receive aptitudes in accordance with our abilities. And what would that mean? It doesn't make sense!

If we want to interpret the parable, then we need to understand the relationship between the talents given and our abilities to receive them. They have a relationship that is only appreciated once understood.

The talents talked about in the parable are the "opportunities" that God gives each servant. Money provides many opportunities. God provides us with many opportunities proportionate to our abilities to love, many of which don't have a monetary value.

For some time, I thought that the wealth or talents were the

---

[72] Cf. Matthew 25:15

mercy and grace that God wants to give each of us. But this led me into blindly acting like the Pharisee in God's Temple judging all sinners a stone's throw away because I thought I was more spiritual.

Some people believe that they receive plenty of opportunities while others think they receive less. Some are very grateful, while others are ungrateful. It is not that God loves some more than others – there is no partiality with God.[73] The reason for the discrepancy in the amount of talents given each servant is because every person has different abilities. The way we view our abilities and our opportunities can lead to judgment, pride, anger, hatred, jealousy, smugness, self-pity, envy, contempt, and insensitivity when we choose darkness, or to practicing humility with God's help when we become noble.

The way we view what God has given us determines whether we react or act with pride or humility.

The ability to react or act can both grow or diminish depending on where the softness and hardness is in one's heart. Softness in the heart belongs to those who practice humility in that area. Hardness in the heart belongs to those who are proud in that area. We all have soft spots and hard spots in our hearts.

The ability to receive or reject these opportunities can and do fluctuate with the different seasons in our lives. We may start out with small opportunities and eventually have a rich

---

[73] Cf. Acts 10:34, Romans 2:11, and Ephesians 6:9

harvest; we may start out with many opportunities but squander many of them. Both prosperous and difficult times can stunt our capitalizing on our opportunities. But can also provide great opportunities for gain. The ability to value the riches or opportunities that God wants to give us, and that the Gospel speaks about, is different with each person.

The parable generally states that those with more talents or "opportunities" will love more than those with fewer talents or "opportunities." But not always! Put another way, those who think they are shown plenty of mercy and grace will more likely share out of that goodness with others. Also, those who view themselves as having been shown less mercy and grace are less likely to shower that mercy and grace on others. The reason for this is that when humans love with supernatural love, they are doing so out of thankfulness for what God has done for them. They aren't trying to earn God's love by doing good deeds.

The parable of the Talents has not been a stagnant pool for me. I have gradually garnished fresh insights from it over the years. I have wondered: what constitutes many talents or huge opportunities, and what constitutes fewer talents or smaller opportunities? I have concluded that huge opportunities involve big risks, lots of pain and suffering, lots of struggles, and that over many years. While small opportunities involve less pain, less struggle, less suffering over smaller time periods. The whole thing is upside down compared to the way the world sees things. And, if we don't understand this we will very easily fall into envy, self-pity, anger, bitterness, meanness, and judgmentalism.

This parable is not about earning God's love. Instead it is about doing things in thankfulness for what God has already done for us. The abilities that we have to make the most of the opportunities that come our way are a response to the love, grace and mercy that God lavishes on us if we have received them from God. If we have yet to know God's mercy and grace, yet live by the Golden Rule: "Do to others what we want them to do to us..."[74] then we will also make the most of every opportunity that comes our way. Any other interpretation would lead to the wrong conclusion that God's salvation can be earned. We are not doing things to take from God; we are doing things because we know the meanings of love, mercy, and grace and give it to people, and desire it for ourselves too.

Those who invest in others the love, mercy, and grace they are granted by God show that they are taking hold of the salvation that God offers them. It means that they don't just handle this gift from God for a while and later bury it, but instead they continually handle the gift through meditation, prayer, and healthy actions. The people who persevere at doing this show that they value God's gifts. Those who start out with God's grace but don't persevere with investing it show that they don't value it enough to hold on to its source.

And of course, Jesus warns us of the just consequences of not taking hold of and investing our ability to dispense mercy and

---

[74] Luke 16:31

grace (shown us by God) in our neighbors' lives when the opportunities show themselves. We get what we choose.

Another reason I think that this parable is about humility and pride is as follows. Consider the words that were spoken by the servant who, when asked by his master (God) why he had done nothing with the gift he was given, said:

> I knew that you are a hard man [God], harvesting where you have not sown and gathering where you have not scattered seed. So, I was afraid and went out and hid your talent in the ground. See, here is what belongs to you.[75]

The servant thought that his master didn't favor him because he had only received a few talents or "opportunities". In the servant's eyes, the other servants had seemingly received more than himself. He was envious of the other servants, and angry with God for not seemingly granting him more goodies. Humble people are thankful for the gifts given to them, and thank those who do the giving.

Pride is not only found in those who seemingly have everything, but also in those who seemingly have nothing.

Note, the servant who did nothing with the opportunities God gave Him said he knew God was hard hearted. The Scriptures say that those who come to God must believe that He is good and a rewarder of those who seek Him[76]. So, it was a lack of faith in this lazy servant that kept him from living out God's

---

[75] Matthew 25:24-25
[76] Hebrews 11:6, & 1 John 1:5

meaningful opportunities for him.

The servant had a broken relationship with God. And out of his fear he built his inner life on fear which resulted in "the tree of knowledge of good and evil" within him having prominence over the opportunities God gave him. For a development and understanding of this tree see this footnote[77].

When people receive riches, they need to invest them. Investing our abilities in the opportunities or "talents" God gives us involves following the Lord Jesus' example and showing care, compassion, love, mercy, and grace to those the Lord leads us to. This will create room in our hearts for the Spirit of God, and we will grow in the certainty of God's goodness. We will come to see that God is for us and not against us. And God's investment will have yielded a faith that imitates God's faithfulness.

A Warning:

It is so easy to fall into the error of judging others when one thinks one understands the Parable of the Talents as discussed above. One might begin to think that others deserve judgment when compared to us, and that we have earned our favor from God by doing the good works that have come because of our opportunities. Jesus warned us to not be like the Pharisee in the Temple who listed his virtues in prayer to God and in the process judged a tax collector a

---

[77] Rene Lafaut, *Dismantling the Tree of Knowledge of Good and Evil Within so Love Can Thrive*

stone's throw away to be worse than he was.[78] Also, we are all on different learning curves. When we see people asking questions that we have already asked and found answers to, it should not become an opportunity for us to become impatient, proud, and judgmental towards them. People who have questions want to learn and show their humility by asking questions. People who have no questions may be proud, closed minded, and unteachable.

Practicing Humility in Community:

Practicing humility in our interior lives allows us to practice it in community. Since humility is not only about how we see ourselves, but how we see others, people who grow in humility will forever be pulling specks or branches out of their own eyes. When this happens there will be an increase in the quality or healthiness of their love towards others gradually, gradually, and then gradually. Observable growth that is slow is the healthiest to experience.

People who see themselves as being independent to the degree that they don't see their dependence on God and society are blind and proud. They are also the ones who will turn a cold shoulder to those who are having difficult times making ends-meat. They are slow to see that there are those who will always be financially dependent on the good will of others. Living in community means that we give and receive, not take and deny.

People who see themselves as being more independent than

---

[78] Luke 18:10

inter-dependent do so because they see themselves as being strong. They don't realize that many other people are much weaker, or less privileged than they were or are. They have never suffered enough to know their own need of mercy. And if they have suffered, it may have hardened their hearts. I know my heart grew hard from self-induced suffering as a child because of my pride, conceit, anger, self-pity, selfishness, and judging.

People who don't practice mercy do so because they don't see themselves in need of mercy. When difficult things happen to them they will not humble themselves. They will steal, take, demand, or commit suicide because they can't bear the shame of being a beggar. They have never given out of love, so they don't know what it is to thankfully receive. And if they do get something good given to them, they often believe they deserve it.

The Golden Rule given by Jesus: "Do to others what you would want others to do to you,"[79] is hardly practiced by proud people. No fallen human being fully practices this rule; we are all proud in some ways. Lord, please have mercy on me a sinner. If one sees oneself as being better than certain groups of people whether because of spiritual, behavioral, physical, know-how, understanding, monitory, moral, sexual, ethnic, or racial lines one has plenty of pride. And Jesus said that the measure we use is the measure that will be measured out to us (Lord Jesus, please have mercy on me a sinner). Humble people see other people as being just as

---

[79] Luke 16:31

important to love as themselves. Humble people are merciful. They are willing to die if necessary for others.

If we give only to those who resemble us, and withhold from those who are different, then we are proud. Jesus said, "But many who are first will be last, and many who are last will be first."[80] If we consider ourselves last, but are envious of others who we consider first, then we really consider ourselves first.

Thinking that we know better than God does when it comes to some or all of the issues pertaining to our lives is another form of pride. Every fallen human being will encounter this kind of pride in his or her heart regularly. Who are we to think that our plans are more important than God's plans? If we do think that our plans are more important than God's plans, then we have either forgotten who God is, or are blind to whom He is in an area. Humility remembers how God has revealed Himself and hungers for more of Him.

People of faith throughout human history have believed that God knows what is best for us. This is because they see God as having unfathomable power, intelligence, understanding and knowledge; as well as being infinitely good, utterly merciful, unsurpassed in compassion, and infinitely wise.

Humble people are growing dependent on God. They value what God has to say, and use His commands (in a caring way) to build the fabric of their lives through His grace.

What Kind of Humility Do We Have?

---

[80] Matthew 19:30

For me humility is attitude showing itself in actions. It moves from darkness to light, and from light to the Light. It moves from confusion to meaning, and from meaning to understanding. It moves from lies to truth, and from truth to the Truth. It moves from hypocrisy to truth. It moves from not caring to caring. It moves from evil to love. It moves from being spiritually unhealthy to health. It moves from idea to action. It searches for lost treasure; treasure that lasts. It cares for the weak, the despised, and the unwanted (Lord please have mercy on me a sinner). Humility knows it has not arrived; humility is not an "all" or "nothing" thing, we can have a little bit of humility, or generous amounts in certain areas of our lives. But we must not let pride swallow its conception, birth, growth, and maturity.

Perhaps the most startling difference between humility and pride is in what they seek. Humility seeks love, relationship, kindness, and respect. Pride seeks power, control, and glory. Humility seeks substance; pride seeks outward appearance alone. There is no greater peace than when humility builds relationships and respect through love. There is no greater discord than when a person mixes pride with power. Humble people can submit to authority, while proud people conceal their rebellion until the opportune time.

If you are uncertain as to whether you are seeking love or power out of humility or pride respectively, ask yourself the following questions:

☐ Am I always seeking to be higher on the totem pole

than everyone else? Am I competing with others even when they are not competing with me? Am I always trying to win? Do I hate losing? Do I covet titles such as apostle, pastor, intelligent, elder, wise, father, mother, doctor, president, or the like more because it looks good than because I enjoy serving in those capacities?

☐ Do I see myself as most important? Do I judge other people with the attitude that I'm better than them?

☐ Am I trying to convince God to make me smarter, faster, stronger, or more creative? Am I envious and unloving towards those who do have these more in abundance than I do? Or in other words, am I looking or searching for power? Do I look down on those who don't seem as intelligent as I am and ask questions with obvious answers?

☐ Do I seek Biblical knowledge more than wanting to be close to God?

☐ Do I seek any knowledge more than knowing people? In doing so, am I impatient with people?

☐ Am I so preoccupied with my own agenda, that I'm impatient with, uncaring, and blind to the humanity belonging to others? Am I mean when my expectations are not met? Am I demanding my rights over other people's rights. Do I have a well-fixed sense of entitlement?

☐ Do I love things, experiences, or concepts more than loving people?

☐ Do I have problems allowing those closest to me to be themselves? Or, is my life a mess, but still I put all my effort in to judging and attempting to change others while totally neglecting myself? Am I impatient with others?

- [ ] Am I envious of other people's success?
- [ ] Do I not trust God enough to generously give to those in need?
- [ ] Do I treat money as God, and God like Money? Do I worship money, and attempt to use God?
- [ ] Do I constantly complain about other people's behaviors? Do I break easily — do I hold resentments, and let the sun go down on my anger regularly and with ease?
- [ ] Am I blind to my pride?
- [ ] Do I think that I am humble enough?
- [ ] Do I have a hard time listening to other peoples' advice?
- [ ] Am I quick to judge other people's ideas as inferior to my own? Do I laugh at, think I see through their agendas, do I ridicule, or scoff at those who try to contribute or care enough to give?
- [ ] When it comes to Jesus' teaching as described in the Bible do I think that I know better?
- [ ] Do I respect people in God-ordained positions of authority, or do I continually fight, complain, protest, and argue with them or against them in an un-respectful manner?
- [ ] Do I always have an "us vs. them" mentality? Do I criticize, blackball, or try to harden the hearts of my listeners towards those belonging to other denominations, or spiritual traditions?
- [ ] Am I more drawn to being served than serving others?

☐ Am I more drawn to worldly success than helping my neighbors? Am I impatient with them?

☐ Do I only have superficial relationships?

☐ Am I always getting into personality conflicts?

☐ Do I try to change others with force (think blackmailing, or using heavy handed approaches) and threats?

☐ Do I have bitterness in my heart and difficulty forgiving others? Do I refuse to forgive others or even just one person?

☐ Do I use anger and self-pity to get my own way?

☐ Do I take things from others instead of graciously receiving them when they are properly offered and God says it is okay?

☐ Do I feel like I always get less than my share of the goodies being handed out? Am I nursing self-pity as a result?

☐ Am I having difficulty accepting God's will for my life?

☐ Am I only interested in pleasure and not truth?

☐ Am I unthankful to God for some of the things that have been given to me?

☐ Do I tackle tasks that are too big for me regularly, and never learn from my mistakes? Do I despise small beginnings?

☐ Do I refuse to take responsibility for the bad things I have done?

☐ Do I feel a "coldness", a motion towards distancing myself, or a pouting attitude towards those who don't receive or applaud my opinions or workmanship the way I desire them to be received? Am I conceited?

☐ Do I always have to be right? Do I feel wounded when my opinions are not well received? Do I struggle with conceit?

☐ Do I see getting my opinions across as being more important than loving others?

☐ Do I look down on others? Do I criticize other people, thinking that I would not do what they do? Do I think I am wise and wouldn't do the 'foolish' things other people have done?

☐ Do I flatter others in order to look good in their eyes more than to love them?

☐ Am I contemptuous?

☐ Do I covet my reputation more than doing the will of God through helping people?

☐ Do I see voicing intense hatred for immorality as a virtue and a sign of my own righteousness?

☐ Do I think about myself too much, and not about what others want (as well as God)? We don't love God whom we have not seen, if we don't love those we can see.

☐ Do I speak too much about myself when in conversations with others? Or am I too preoccupied with self and refuse to focus on the needs or humanity of others?

☐ Do I try to impress others with my spirituality?

☐ Am I always thinking about what others might be thinking about me, and are moved or motivated out of the fear or pride thereof?

- [ ] Do I handle rejection poorly? Am I very insecure?
- [ ] Do I look more leniently towards my sins than on the sins of others? Do I jump to conclusions quickly...only to realize that I had no perspective in my disputes and land up hurting those involved?
- [ ] Do I care more about how my actions look on the outside than my motives? Am I more caring about whether others are friendly to me than whether I do the right things?
- [ ] Am I no longer teachable? Do I see myself more as a teacher and leader than a follower?
- [ ] Do I see myself as not having to ask God for the things I need because I view myself as independent, self-sufficient, and rich?

We will all say, "Yes" to at least some of these questions some of the time, and so seek power more than humility and love in some area in each of our lives. If you answer, "Yes" to many of these questions then you definitely seek power more than love as a goal in your life. If while reading the above you were thinking mostly how it applied to someone else you know, then you might be either very observant or in denial about your own flaws. I don't mean for anyone to be condemned by this list or to become focused on this list. It is meant more as a diagnostic tool. There is help[81] on how to kill our strongholds of pride and lack of love in our lives.

The more we focus on sin the more we will get drawn into it. Only by abiding in Jesus (to grow in humility) will we start to

---

[81] Cf. Rene Lafaut, *Dismantling the Tree of Knowledge of Good and Evil Within So Love Can Thrive*

have victory over pride. Abiding in Jesus means we start to grow humble attitudes, and become teachable in a way that leads to gentleness, love, and respect.

Four Categories of People:

Here they are:

(1) Those people who with the good found in them see themselves not in need of God.

(2) Those people who are drawn to the good within them and pursue God for more believing what they have is not enough.

(3) Those people because of the bad found within them don't want anything to do with God because they are happy with the pleasures and evil to be found in the world.

(4) Those people who because of the bad within themselves hunger for purity and so pursue God.

Admittedly there is a bit of each of these in each fallen human being. One tendency might be stronger than any other depending on the person. But there is hope for each of us.

15 JESUS THE WAY THE TRUTH AND THE LIFE

Ultimately each of our attitudes will fall somewhere on the continuum between pride and humility. The critical mass of humility that is required for salvation is when God who is Love is allowed to touch the soul so supernatural love is birthed in the person. We love supernaturally not out of ourselves, but because God first loves us.

And by supernatural love, I mean the kind that is described in the Bible. Love doesn't try to earn God's favor. It is inspired, does things out of thankfulness to God, and does so because it cares for other people.

People who have never verbally heard the Good News about Jesus' love can still have this critical mass of humility. In John's Gospel, it talks about Jesus being:

> The true light that gives light to every man.[82]

Light is a metaphor for goodness and love. So, Jesus not only puts natural love in each person's heart at conception, but is of good will towards each person. Some people's natural loves are greater than other people's supernatural loves. If one believes in the Light even though one doesn't know its true name, then one still believes in the same God as healthy Christians do. Believing in the light means that one respects God and does what is right to the best of one's ability. The story of Cornelius in the book of Acts in chapter 10 bears this

---

[82] John 1:9

out.

People like Cornelius consistently choose to have mercy on others, because they know that they themselves need mercy. And Jesus said that because they do this they would be shown mercy. When the Gospel is presented to them they eventually come to believe.

This does not mean that everyone is going to go to Heaven. Cranking out moral behavior and mentally agreeing with a few correct doctrines and thinking that by them we earn or win Heaven will not get us Heaven. Heaven is a gift not a wage. Those who eventually do enter Heaven do so because Jesus forgives their sins. Those people still on earth that do love, do sin every now and then. God forgives us freely, but the forgiveness needs to be received by us when we become aware of His offer, for it to do its work in us and restore our friendships with God. Jesus showed His love for all of us by dying on a cross because of the sin in all of us, and it is this sin that still wants to kill Him. All we need to do is to accept Him as Lord and Savior and then follow Him.

In humbling ourselves we invite God into our lives because God is close to the humble but far from proud people. Proud people are holding onto earthly treasures because that is where their security and life are found. So long as they hold onto wealth, power, and misguided loyalties instead of God they don't have the kind of humility that brings grace into their hearts. Out of humility we can have a relationship with Jesus and therefore be saved/ healed/ and forgiven our sins. Those who follow the Light (Jesus/ God) will not see the darkness of hell or the lake of fire. This is true even if they have never heard someone speak the name "Jesus" to them before. If this is so, then they know God by some other name. They may have many errors in their doctrines and beliefs. Who doesn't? But they practice humility to the best of their knowledge. Psalm 149:4 says that God crowns the humble with salvation. Practicing Christians are not the only ones who have a critical amount of humility here on earth.

Spiritually thirsty people search for life giving drink. We are all thirsty, but some of us just don't know that we are thirsty for God. Some people drink poison or lies that lead them to idol worship thinking that such things will give them life (many Christians have done or still do this). Proud or foolish, blind, rich people mistake what gives life and what gives death, and won't change even when the genuine thing is offered to them. Often they are addicted to the idols, and this requires grace to be set free from.

One of the most controversial and misunderstood sayings from Jesus is:

> I am the way and the truth and the life. No-one comes to the Father except through me.[83]

When Jesus says that He is the way, it means that we must follow Him when invited, if we want to see the Father. It also means that we must seek to imitate Him in His humility if we are to follow Him, because He is humble, and we can't walk together unless we are agreed.

---

[83] John 14:6

When Jesus says that He is the truth it means that He won't deceive us. It also means that He will help us die to our hypocrisy if we are willing. Hypocrisy is rooted in pride. Truth also sets free: Jesus sets free. Unfortunately, we can get tangled up so easily because of our guilt, fear and pride.

When Jesus said that He is the life, He means that we will find true non-hypocritical life in Him by us abiding in Him so that He will empower us to do what He taught in the Sermon on the Mount.[84] We won't be disappointed with what he offers because He made us for Himself. It also means that through His passion and sacrifice on the cross and subsequent Resurrection, He has opened the door to fellowship with the Father for us. We take hold of this life when we have a change of mind and believe in the Light (Jesus).

If we think that we can practice humility without the Light, then we deceive ourselves. If we could practice humility without the Jesus, then what do we indeed see with without the light?

A lot of people have problems with Jesus being the only way. But how many of these people would quarrel with God's way as being the only way? If Jesus weren't God, then He couldn't be the only way. His way means to humble ourselves and follow the light that He has given us. Jesus can save anonymously; the church is not the only way to Heaven, but Jesus is.

In dying on the cross and resurrecting from the dead Jesus

---

[84] Cf. Matthew 5:1-7:29, or Luke 6:20-6:49

became mankind's Judge and Savior for all time as well as on the Last Day. When Jesus judges on the Last Day He will dispense mercy to multitudes of people who had never heard the Good News verbally before. Those whom He has mercy on will have peace with God through Him as Judge and Savior. Hence, "No-one comes to the Father except through Jesus."

For those who have heard about Jesus and His deeds, He invites us to learn to love God, self and people when He says:

> Come to me, all you who are weary and burdened, and I will give you rest. Take my yoke upon you and learn from me, for I am gentle and humble in heart, and you will find rest for your souls. For my yoke is easy and my burden is light.[85]

To learn how to love takes growing in the practice of humility. Take on His yoke – His teachings, promises, and presence that comes from believing the Good News as described in the Gospels! You won't be disappointed if what you are seeking is to love and be loved.

Rest in His Love and forgiveness by accepting His unconditional love which is His grace.

---

[85] Matthew 11:28-30

16 TO BE BORN FROM ABOVE OR AGAIN?

What I would like to do in this Chapter is to describe what it means to be born again or to be born from above.

It is not a one-time event. Rather it is a process that normally extends from a beginning point and ends in Heaven. The beginning point occurs when one comes out of spiritual darkness and starts to walk in a marvelous light (LOVE). Just like a baby in a womb is in darkness and isolated from others, when it comes out of the darkness into the light it starts to form relationships. In the spiritual, living relationships are based on connection, warmth, love, mercy, and grace. So, when one starts to be born from above, one starts a relationship with God based on what Jesus Christ did 2000-years ago (which is and was His unending LOVE) whether one realizes it or not.

There are two steps to being born from above. And they are summarized in the Old Testament saying, "In repentance and rest is your salvation."[86] The invitation is to repent, meaning to have a change of mind, and then to rest one's faith in God, the Light, or Jesus. Repenting is always done in prayer, in God's presence. We don't clean ourselves off and then go into God's presence. There is rubber meets the road help[87] on how to repent.

Both a commitment to repentance, and resting one's faith in

---

[86] Isaiah 30:15

[87] Cf. Rene Lafaut, *Dismantling the Tree of Knowledge of Good and Evil Within So Love Can Thrive*

Jesus Christ are vows that one normally makes at one's Baptism. And that is why the New Testament says that our Baptisms save us, provided we continue to hold onto God's love with faith in Jesus with a clean conscience.

Full repentance means that one eventually turns away (with Jesus' help) from whatever Jesus calls sin, and instead one begins to humbly love God, one's enemies, and oneself just like Jesus teaches us to do in the Sermon on the Mount in Matthew's Gospel.[88] One can't truly repent without the help of God. Repentance requires that we cooperate with God so that He can clean us up from our guilt and sinful actions. It requires faith, caring for people, patiently knocking on all the doors on the way, and persevering in the love learning curve.

To rest one's faith in Jesus means that one begins to trust in His sacrificial love shown on the cross 2000-years ago, His Resurrection from the dead, and His continual leadership/ shepherding/ and Kingship over us in the present.

---

[88] Cf. Matthew 5:1-7:29, or Luke 6:20-6:49

17 THE FINAL JUDGMENT

Truth is not always pleasant to the ears. I wish no one would die. Yet, people die every day. I wish no one lied. Yet, all people do lie. I wish there were no experiences known as Hell or the Lake of Fire. Whether these names refer to real places or are metaphors for certain types of suffering people undergo in the afterlife I don't know, but I do believe at a minimum that they are states of existence.

Hell is not the only place of torment. There is also the Lake of Fire. In the end those who find themselves in a state of Hell will enter the Lake of Fire as their final destination.

Many don't want to believe in Hell or the lake of fire. As far as I can see, if there is pain in this life then there are no guarantees to all that there won't be pain in the next life. There is grace for those who are open to it. But God can't force His grace onto unwilling people. That doesn't mean that God condemns people to Hell or the Lake of Fire; people condemn themselves to be there. God has come to save us in the person of Jesus Christ. Only Satan comes to kill, steal, and destroy. Jesus hates sin, death, and decay. He came to save us from them. Jesus did not come to save us from God the Father's wrath. He came to save us from our sins, and sin's intrinsic consequences, especially death. Sin kills us; not God. Sin mutilates/ decays/ and infects the image of God we are made in. Sin causes guilt, and guilt if not forgiven or relieved rightly causes the worst kind of suffering, insecurity, and paranoia in the end; and that might be in my opinion what

Hell and the Lake of Fire are all about. Sin pushes God away from us, but His presences is Heaven, so in pushing Him away we push life and peace away from us too because He is life and His presence is peace.

For those who hear the Spirit speak to them and change their minds and believe in Jesus, grace is given that enables them to be saved from sin and sin's consequences, the worst being death.

> In being forgiven sin we have guilt removed.
> In renewing our minds and hearts we are born again.
> These bring health (or holiness) and love for God, others, and self.
> This is a consequence of life, mercy and grace.
> This is Heaven, this is life.

> In refusing to be forgiven we struggle with guilt, and insecurity,
> and have identity issues.
> Our minds and hearts feel stagnant, lifeless, and at a dead end.
> These bring the feelings of despair, shame, hopelessness, apathy and hatred.
> Such are the consequences of sin.
> This is death or Hell.

Is there a state or place named Hell? Yes, I do believe so, but my beliefs or understanding of its purpose has radically changed over the years.

The idea of retributive Justice used to be very important to me because that is the way I tried to justify Eternal Damnation, but now I think God is into restorative justice. I remind myself how easy it is to lose faith. When people see hypocrisy in faith groups they take a step back and think twice on whether to walk away or not. Because some get disillusioned they refuse to bond with any organization who claims to know the way to Heaven. The news in the New Testament about Hell is about how certain people will experience (a lack of) God in the afterlife. Every good thing God attempts to do for them is seen with skepticism and ill intent. We all to a very large degree create our own realities and somehow manage to live with them.

Hell, in my opinion is a dark place in the minds of those who experience it. Not because God wills it, but because the people there push God away who is Light and warmth. The dark and cold are what they feel when they push God away. The darkness is representative of void, lack of footing, no foundation, or more to the point: fear, insecurity, and the trepidation of not having received the forgiveness of one's sins because of what Jesus did on the Cross.

The Lake of Fire is a metaphor for the burning thirst we all have for God that is not met with those there because of pride, and having tried to only satisfy it by idols (that are no longer available). In the New Testament, it says that an axe is set to every tree that does not bear good fruit. Have you ever been cut by a piece of paper, or a knife; or scrapped your knee on concrete? It burns horribly, this is the effect that the axe has on those trees (or people) who reject friendship with

God. I believe God says out of justice (not retributive justice), "I need to put an end to the waste of resources because such plants bear me no good fruit" and this cutting off away of resources burns something fierce...this suffering is a torment for those who experience it.

Pride causes the boundary that keeps people in the states or places known as hell or the Lake of Fire. God does not will it. God would embrace these people if they would only humble themselves and open themselves up to God. But they push God away. The NT makes it clear that for some this is Eternal, not because God wills it but because they will it.

There that is my take on Hell and the Lake of Fire.

Jesus makes it clear that we ought not judge or condemn people made in God's image. We are forbidden to take life in the Bible by God. We may not even follow through on giving life when it is in our power to do so. So we ought not be too quick to condemn or take another person's life. Dealing out death and judgment is God's domain because He alone can give life.

I hope that people don't think that I am, "too eager to deal out death in judgment" in writing this book. I am not that wise, and I certainly don't see all ends.

So why choose Jesus? I personally have felt the love, compassion, mercy, discipline, and grace of the historical Jesus as describe in the Christian Bible. Nothing else offers the hope that He does in my opinion.

18 THE PARABLE OF THE PRODIGAL SON

The time came when God finally wanted me to re-examine some of the teaching that I heard at the *Overflowing Grace Conference* by Ken Blue way back in 1992. He wanted me to understand the true meaning of the parable about the prodigal son found in Luke 15:11-32. Here is the parable:

> "There was a man who had two sons. The younger one said to his father, 'Father, give me my share of the estate.' So he divided his property between them.

> "Not long after that, the younger son got together all he had, set off for a distant country and there squandered his wealth in wild living. After he had spent everything, there was a severe famine in that whole country, and he began to be in need. So he went and hired himself out to a citizen of that country, who sent him to his fields to feed pigs. He longed to fill his stomach with the pods that the pigs were eating, but no-one gave him anything.

> "When he came to his senses, he said, 'How many of my father's hired men have food to spare, and here I am starving to death! I will set out and go back to my father and say to him: Father, I have sinned against heaven and against you. I am no longer worthy to be called your son; make me like one of your hired men.' So he got up and went to his father.

> "But while he was still a long way off, his father saw

him and was filled with compassion for him; he ran to his son, threw his arms around him and kissed him.

"The son said to him, 'Father, I have sinned against heaven and against you. I am no longer worthy to be called your son.'

"But the father said to his servants, 'Quick! Bring the best robe and put it on him. Put a ring on his finger and sandals on his feet. Bring the fattened calf and kill it. Let's have a feast and celebrate. For this son of mine was dead and is alive again; he was lost and is found.' So they began to celebrate.

"Meanwhile, the older son was in the field. When he came near the house, he heard music and dancing. So he called one of the servants and asked him what was going on. 'Your brother has come,' he replied, 'and your father has killed the fattened calf because he has him back safe and sound.'

"The older brother became angry and refused to go in. So his father went out and pleaded with him. But he answered his father, 'Look! All these years I've been slaving for you and never disobeyed your orders. Yet you never gave me even a young goat so I could celebrate with my friends. But when this son of yours who has squandered your property with prostitutes comes home, you kill the fattened calf for him!'

" 'My son,' the father said, 'you are always with me, and everything I have is yours. But we had to celebrate

and be glad, because this brother of yours was dead
and is alive again; he was lost and is found.' "

The paraphrase I heard at the Overflowing Grace Conference
of this wonderful real story is something like this:

There were two brothers who were both cranking out
the good behavior until the younger one asks the
father for his inheritance and a day later packs his bags
and heads for a distant country. He squanders his
money, and lands up being hired to feed pigs. He
finally comes to his senses because of his hunger, and
prepares a little speech for his father: "Father I have
sinned against Heaven and against you. I'll crank out
the good behavior in exchange for you taking me back
and feeding me." He then proceeds to return home,
and when he is still far off in the distance His father
sees him and runs off to meet him. The younger son is
embraced by the father, and the son starts to recite his
speech. But the father doesn't listen to the speech. He
gives him a ring, new threads, and holds a banquet in
His child's honor.

The older brother finds out that his dad is holding a
party for his younger brother and won't go in to join in
the festivities. His father comes out to plead with him.
But the older son says, "I have been cranking out the
good behavior all this time, and not once did you hold
a party for me and my friends. Don't you think that I
deserve even that? Yet your younger son goes and
squanders your wealth with prostitutes and look at

how you reward him."

The moral of the story is this. If you want God's grace, then go to Him, don't do more, try harder, or crank out the good behavior to win God over to your side. God loves you whether you sin heavily or lightly. Your sin doesn't determine whether God loves you or not. God loves you because He is love. You can't earn God's favor in one area by doing right in another area.

However, there is one kind of sin that can block God's unconditional love or grace, not because God withholds it, but because it blocks grace. It is pride. Pride leads to judging (among other sins) people all of whom God loves.

I used to judge those people who landed up homeless and addicted to street drugs or alcohol as being very unwise. I thought it would never happen to me because of my "great" wisdom. I now know that this was very pompous, proud, and foolish of me. I now know that it doesn't matter how much moral resolve I have; I can land up living on the streets addicted to drugs or alcohol if the right circumstances are to come along. Yes, there go I but for the grace of God.

The Bible teaches us that we need to trust God for our salvation. He desires it more than we do for our selves.

The prodigal son went back to his father not because he thought his father would be impressed, but because he was hungry for love, joy, and right living. He went hesitantly, knowing how he had treated his father in the past. He did not say, "boy, my father will be impressed and happy to see me"

... if anything he felt ashamed for how he had treated his father... and he felt that it was possible that his father might reject him because of his previous bad behavior. But the Father welcomes him. The Father had greater love than the prodigal remembered or expected. No sin can keep the Father from welcoming back His son when the son through humility seeks out his Father. The prodigal son did not fully say to himself, "boy I am doing a great thing by going back to my father". But he did believe and hope that his dad would accept him based on what he formally had done. He knew though, that the father had a right to reject him just like he had rejected his father.

But the father had always loved the prodigal and was willing to wait until his son figured it out that he still loved him. It was the hope of his father's mercy that prompted the prodigal to find his way home. And it was the love from the Father that brought about renewal for the Prodigal: to leave everything behind and embrace the life that the father had for him. It was the Father's love that motivated and restored the relationship with His son. When the son realized that he was loved unconditionally the relationship was finally healed.

Rightly directed repentance means that I let God be in charge of cleaning me up. Notice, that the father in the above parable gives his younger son new threads, and these new threads are symbolic of repentance that bears good fruit. I don't repent and bear good fruit all by myself (i.e. I don't clean myself up all by myself), and then go into the Father's presence. It is our Father who cleans us up, and that is the result of true repentance. The result of repentance is that I will bear good fruit to the Father's glory.

Notice that there are two parts to rightly directed repentance: (1) I accept God's lavish grace and mercy for me because I have a change of mind about where I'm at spiritually (i.e. I admit I have sinned, and I have sorrow or sadness for the sins I have committed, and then I approach God in faith because of His promises, by humbly confessing my sins to God), and (2) God's response to my plea for mercy (forgiveness) and grace (infilling presence and cleansing me) making me clean and holy (healthy) in conscience and action over time through strategic prayer, renewing my mind and growing in dependence on Jesus to save us from sin and enable us to love more deeply.

Notice that the prodigal son is so poor that he can't even change his own rags for good clothing, but he humbles himself and goes in faith and out of hope for his Father's mercy and grace anyways. And the Father lavishes that grace on His child.

Another important point is that the prodigal son was a child of the father because the father had fathered him: not because the son was ever worthy. So, the statement by the prodigal that he no longer was worthy to be a son is "literally" incorrect, because the son never earned the right of sonship. But it does point to the son's admission that he does not deserve the privileges of being a son. Before the prodigal asked for his inheritance he was not worthy to be a son of the father. However, he had worth in the father's eyes.

Conception and birth come before behavior. God's love comes before our behaviors. Our good behaviors ought to flow from God's life, love, and presence. They do flow from Him when we aren't using them to impress Him or others, or are attempting to get stuff from Him or others and not really caring for Him or them.

Many people feel they only want God's blessings because they don't like their quiet times with God. This is sad because the devil has lied to them about who God is and what they can expect from Him in their quiet times. Yes, our quiet times can feel boring, useless, dry, empty, and a waste of time but not always. Yet, the devil will try to use this uncomfortableness to get us to quit. Spending time in the presence of God no matter how it feels tells God that He matters, and is key to getting to know Him better instead of prayer just being about myself. When we learn two-way journaling, our Quiet times will then be able to flourish.

19 WHY I BELIEVE GOD WANTED JESUS TO DIE FOR US

I do not believe in the Penal Substitution Theory of the Atonement. Our ugly sinful malice and hatred put Jesus on the cross; not God's wrath. The god that breathes fire at one's least infraction and needs to punish his son on a tree just to vent his wrath so he could accept us is the way a lot of people see God. I would call this cosmic child abuse if it were true. Reading much from those who studied the early Church Fathers and reading about the history of Penal Substitution Theory I am forced to reject it as the way I personally explain the cross and redemption. I know that the way we see god/ God determines the kind of people we are going to become.

There are many mysteries, stories, and intrigues that have stuff hidden from even the most informed people. I think the same is true about Salvation History. As far as in the beginning in the Garden of Eden, all the motives, loyalties, longings, thoughts, and desires that went through Adam and Eve's minds and hearts, and where God stood at the time has not been clearly or fully revealed. With that said finding motivation for Jesus Passion can be tricky. I'm grateful to a Bible Study I attended for challenging me, correcting, and giving me focus on this important topic: The Atonement. They accept the Penal Substitution Theory in this area, whereas I don't, but they made some very good and healthy points that I now accept and which have brought stability to my mind and peace to my heart.

I see Jesus' Passion, Crucifixion and Resurrection as a rescue mission orchestrated by the Trinity. With the Father in love (not anger) giving the Son to the world. The Son, Jesus, who knew no sin, entered "death" so He could absorb those people (who died in friendship with God) into Himself, so that when He rose from the dead (because death could not hold Him) those in Him would be made alive to newness of life. This solves the sin-problem for those who died in friendship with God. Jesus came to solve the sin problem. Also, for those who are still alive, when they are baptized into Jesus death through faith they are raised up into newness of life through Jesus' Resurrection (Cf. First Peter 3:21).

The new life (the Holy Spirit and grace) that we receive from Jesus through faith in His Life, Passion/ and Resurrection are meant to fortify us against sin. Jesus came to save us from our sins and the consequences of sin, not His Father' wrath (Matthew 1:21). Nowhere in the Gospels does it say that God punished Jesus for our sins with (infinite) wrath. It does say that we punished Jesus for speaking the truth. No one can buy love. Jesus did not purchase God the Father's love for us. It was the Father's love that brought Jesus to us. God is not mean, petty, eye-for-eye tooth-for-tooth revengeful in His countenance towards us, or anyone else.

Many people wrongly read Penal Substitution into the many Bible Scriptures (OT and NT) that talk about Jesus dying for us and our sins. I think these verses are talking about Jesus rescuing us from our sins and their consequences. I whole heartedly believe that Jesus came to save us from our sins. He came to save us from further losing the image of God we were created in and to restore it fully. The worst thing that can happen to us is to lose the image of God that we were created with. There are many different theories on how the Atonement could possibly work. Penal substitution was not a view held by the early Church Fathers, and the way it is presented in Evangelical Churches started with the Reformation with people like Calvin.

Here[89] are some of those verses that people who accept the Penal Substitution Theory of the Atonement use to try support their view.

I think these verses can easily be interpreted with the view that Jesus came to win our sanctification and was willing to pay for it with the pain and punishment we inflicted on Him because we didn't want to hear the truth, at least initially.

In the NT[90] it says that Jesus was crucified from the foundation of the world. If that is true, and one believes in the Penal Substitution View of the Atonement, does that mean God was punishing Jesus for our sins from the foundation of the world? I don't think so. So, I reject the PST of the Atonement.

Can anyone buy your love? If yes, is it still love? Can anyone buy God the Father's love? If yes, then it isn't love. Jesus did not buy out God, so that God could love us. I therefore reject

---

[89] Isaiah 53:4-6, 10-11, Romans 3:23-26, 2 Corinthians 5:21, Galatians 3:10,13, 1 Peter 2:24, 1 Peter 3:18
[90] Cf. Revelations 13:8

the PST of the atonement.

Penal Substitution motivates itself by saying that God is both Love and Holy. The holiness part is defined by some-kind-of "vague" unknowable "separated-ness". And it is this separated-ness that supposedly demands payment for sins by punishment. This payment was supposedly received from Jesus and inflicted by God the Father (but God did not join us in our hostility towards Jesus on the cross). I ask, aren't we all commanded to live holy lives ourselves (Cf. 1 Peter 1:16)? Isn't our holiness supposed to reflect God's holiness? If so, then we ought to punish people when they sin against us because our holiness means we must reflect God's holiness in the Penal Substitution Theory of the Atonement, if it were true. But we are not allowed to hurt others for hurting us, instead, we are to forgive. I rather like to think holiness means to be spiritual healthy, staying away from sin, being separated from evil, darkness, and hatred, and instead being devoted to healthy love. God has this kind of holiness, and we are commanded to pursue it in the Bible. This kind of holiness does not demand punishment immediately when sin happens (Cf. Matthew 5:5,7). It longs for reconciliation, willingly forgives, heals, and is into restorative Justice from the get go (Jesus came to undo the works of the devil not to finish the devil's work (Cf. 1 John 3:8)).

There are usually two forms of justice that are spoken about: restorative and retributive. I think there is a third: putting an end to injustices. We all deserve the consequences of our sins, but that doesn't mean we should relish it when people reap the horrible consequences that they sow. Sin is bad, and sin along with sin's consequences are the punishments for sin. Jesus, God the Father, and the Holy Spirit don't delight in the death of the wicked. God is not mean, and does not meanly punish anyone.

The places where Jesus gets angry in the Gospels are not where He is hateful of the people He is angry with. When Jesus tells parables where the bad guy gets his due He is not saying He hates the bad guy, He is saying He hates what the bad guy did. Jesus is slow to anger, but when the sin has run its course in rebellion hurting people and rejecting God's pleas all the way, God wants to put an end to it for justice sake. Often people think there are only two kinds of justice: restorative and retributive. God however, is gentle and meek. Justice also means putting an "end" to an injustice. Those who dislike the "end-results that come their way" when God stops the show, see it as retributive because the party has come to an end for them. Whatever happens after the injustice is stopped, will depend on the attitudes of those involved in the situation. God can give people over to their sins, or He can restore them. No amount of punishment is going to undo the injustice. Only God is able to save, heal and forgive fully.

The main reason Jesus died a cruel slow death was to show His love for us (not to appease the anger of a supposedly blood thirsty wrathful God). He died for you and me, for your sins and mine. He showed that He was willing to suffer excruciating pain (that led to death) for us while at the same time resisting any way out even though He could have ended it at any moment before or during His suffering took place. He wanted to show that He is willing to die for each of us so He could show just how great His love for us was and is. If we aren't willing to die for another person we can't possibly love them that much. Jesus did die for us and therefore showed His love for us to the fullest possible extent.

For a long time, I had a poorly informed understanding of why Jesus died through His Passion. In those days, I believed that Jesus became totally separated from and experienced the wrath of God the Father so that He could pay the penalty for our sins. But I'd later come to see that this was downright misguided in many ways even contradicting sacred Scripture.

I used to think that there was something "just" about Jesus being crucified because I got the word "flesh" confused with the word "body". I saw His "flesh" crucified on the cross as symbolic of our "body", "flesh" or "sin nature", that needed (past and present (continuous tense)) to be killed so that we could somehow be done with the dark side of our humanity. So, I saw our bodies as evil. But the human body is good not evil. It is not responsible for our "flesh" or "sin nature" that seeks to corrupt us. Even though Jesus' body was crucified, it did not kill our "sin nature". Jesus did not and has not a "sin nature" and His body was completely healthy. This bad theology leads to giving the "sin nature" more power and influence in one's life than it needs.

Now it is true that Christ died for our sins, so that we would not have to be separated from God forever in the Lake of

Fire. But it is not true that God the Father vented His wrath on Jesus for our sake. The Son was, is, and will forever be precious to God the Father, and that means that He was also precious to Him during the Passion. God the Father has always loved the Son, and the Son has always loved the Father. Christ's Sacrifice on the cross was a sweet aroma to the Father, and pleased the Father because the act was done in utter and complete selflessness, that is, was done in absolute love. Jesus did what Adam failed to do. But that does not mean that Jesus was obligated to correct Adam's mistake. Isaiah 53 says Jesus' Passion was a travesty of justice meaning He owed us nothing. Yet it is true that Jesus suffered so we would not have to, but not by what some call "penal substitution" or "retributive justice."

A benefit that comes from Jesus dying comes from the old proverb: "You can't judge a person until you have walked in her or his shoes." The only fitting judge is Jesus because He died a cruel death without sinning that gives Him insight into our conditions, compassion for our situations, and solidarity with us in all our sufferings, temptations, and trials.

Jesus became savior and judge through enduring a passion and death without sin.

Jesus died for us as we humanity vented our poison on Him through His Passion, and He absorbed the poison of hatred, evil, pride, judging, meanness, contempt, hostility, cynicism, and anger in us as we directed it at Him, and He in the process can and does heal us. We are truly healed by Jesus' stripes.

In a very mysterious way Jesus paid that price for us through His passion. But it must be emphasized that God is not like demon spirits that in the past demanded children-sacrifices through fires in order to appease the demon's anger and grant safety or prosperity or acceptance to those sacrificing the children.

God can and does forgive freely, lovingly, compassionately, and mercifully; and has tied forgiveness to the cross for many reasons many of which are still hidden to us. The cross is a mystery that draws us in wonder to behold God's love for us. God is not the "accountant type of god" who somehow needs to balance the books when it comes to the weight of our sins and Jesus' suffering. With the thinking that He can't give us freedom unless somebody proportionally loses it.

God wanted to show how strong His love is for us: He was willing to hang on a cross and die to express that love. An added benefit from this is that we have a perfect example to imitate when it comes to sacrificial, and enemy love.

Jesus' cross (along with all our own crosses) represents our call to love. Jesus calls us to pick up our own crosses (accept our circumstances) and to follow Him each day. Love is sacrificial in nature. It can be a hard thing to do some of the time (making it so sought after and celebrated), so Jesus leads the way in showing us what love looks like by being our example even though He is not inclined towards sin. Jesus helps us to focus on love; not self. We are called to be love-centered; not self-centered.

When we believe in Jesus as Savior and Leader (or Lord) we

become a part of the Bride of Christ through Baptism. And if we persevere in loyalty and holiness until death, we will inherit the fruits of Jesus' Passion – the beatific vision.

However, that does not mean that as we sojourn here on earth and anticipate Heaven that God has left us to our own devices without cure or remedy to prevent us from committing serious sins endlessly. Indeed, by "Jesus' stripes we are healed"[91] not so much from physical ailments (although that can be a reality), but from the spiritual maladies in our hearts, souls and minds, and relationships.

Jesus fully embraced our humanity on the cross, wounds, scoffing, and weakness. He shows us that we are not alone when we invite Him into our hearts where His grace, warmth, and peace put and end to the old life. These spiritual maladies (such as deception, fear, pride, insensitivity, or addictions) are slowly removed. There is further practical help[92] to become free from compulsions, addictions and character flaws.

The Path that Jesus calls us to walk is difficult. But He has promised to help us persevere through all our trials and promises that these trials are full of opportunities to grow in personal holiness (healthiness), knowledge of God's goodness, and in the skill of love. Jesus by His Passion has shown us the way to reality, to meaningful giving, and to love.

Fact: I have sinned repeatedly, and so in some sense am

---

[91] Isaiah 53:5
[92] Cf. Rene Lafaut, *Dismantling the Tree of Knowledge of Good and Evil Within So Love Can Thrive*

separated from God because of it when I do. Fact: Jesus came and was mutilated in the flesh so I could be healed in my spirit/ soul/ heart/ and mind and not have to be separated from God forever. Fact: God the Father did not punish His Son Jesus Christ through His Passion. Indeed, God was in Christ on the Cross reconciling the world to Himself. Fact: God loves unconditionally, but He does not owe us love.

Thinking we understand the Gospel message should not lead to pride, to thinking we are in the know in such a way where it is "me=(in the know or am better and I'm so clever) vs. them=(ignorant or are foolish and unrighteous)" judgment placed between me and them. The Gospel is about grace, only pride goes against it.

20 MERCY, KARMA, POSITIVITY AND NEGATIVITY[93]

Jesus said, "blessed are the merciful, for they will receive mercy."[94] A dictionary meaning of mercy is "having compassion and forgiveness toward someone who is within our power to punish and harm."

When we are able to empathize with a person who has done us harm we are able to show them more mercy. For example, when someone insults us and rejects us for a simple mistake we made. Then we can hold on to our peace knowing that this person has probably been damaged in the past by just this kind of treatment.

Coming to a place of understanding helps mightily in the process of forgiveness.

The knowledge from God's word that we are all sinners also brings us to a place where we can be merciful in our attitude toward this person. With this open broad acceptance of people, in all walks of life and sin conditions, we can be merciful and receive mercy.

It's a different mindset from those who live by "an eye for an eye and a tooth for a tooth." In their mind, this form of treatment seems perfectly fair. They desire fairness for themselves and fairness in theory for others. But without the compassion inherent in the golden rule it often becomes a cold judgment. A judgment that says: "They should get what

---

[93] Thank you Anita for reworking the content from this chapter
[94] Matthew 5:7

is coming to them."

This type of thinking is behind the concept of karma: If you do bad things to others, bad things will happen to you. If you do good things to others, you will have good things happen to you. It's the idea that in the future, there will be punishment for bad deeds and rewards for good deeds. The trouble is we have all done bad or sinful things. My sins are not better or worse than anyone else's, so it is a level playing field.

We as Christians don't live by "karma"; we live by grace! But we do believe in the powers of positive and negative attitudes. Positivity draws positive stuff, whereas negativity draws negative stuff.

Getting free of judgmental attitudes can bring us to a place of awareness of our own hearts. We become aware of when our attitudes turn to a negative place.

When we are positive, we are strong; not negative and needy. We walk with hope, we are able to conquer the difficulties that come our way. When we are positive and strong, people are actually attracted to us and want to be around us.

We can all learn to handle negative events with hope, positivity, understanding and love. It all depends on our perspective!

The belief in karma can be hard thing to shake. But grace and humility can help us to jettison it.

21 HUMAN KIND

We were all made in the image of God. And since God is wholly good, we are also good, a goodness marred by a "sin nature". This we inherited from our ancestors Adam and Eve. Since we are made in God's image, it means that each one of us is made for God and not for Hell or the Lake of Fire. We are given gifts at our conception: the natural loves that are a preparation for supernatural love that comes from God's Spirit. The emptiness, the darkness, and the death inside of us can only be cured by Jesus who seeks to give His Spirit of life wherever and whenever possible. The emptiness inside of us attracts us to sin, but also to God. Those vacuums within us are destined to be filled with God's supernatural life, but often we fill it with lesser things: idols. Many don't know their spiritual condition. God offers us all supernatural life. But the devil blinds whomever he can deceive. All goodness, beauty, and truth are preparations for the Good News of Jesus Christ. Each person has some goodness, beauty, and truth in them. If they didn't they would not have been created in the image of God.

I personally am learning that I can't judge or condemn any other person because I am not God. My judgments when it comes to judging people is fleshly, I don't have the authority or the grace to judge anyone. When I judge people I always discount them, rob them of their voice, humanity, and dignity in my meanness, and I am drawn to refuse mercy, and box people in. In doing so I judge like the devil does. When we have no wood branches in our eyes, then we can help people to see in healthier ways, but this does not involve judging them it involves correcting them or sharing our pearls of wisdom when invited to. The energies are different: judging is black, whereas being invited to give an opinion in a non-mean way is God's way. God is judge (and He does not judge like the devil, God judges in love). He has left the final judgment to the Last Day to His Only Begotten Son: Jesus. Should I not let Him do the judging? He can have mercy on whomever He chooses. But we can condemn ourselves. May He continue to have mercy on us now and forever more. Amen!

22 DO YOU WANT TO BE A GOOD PERSON?

A truly righteous or humble person is one who means it when they say, "I have sinned" despite what others might say when in fact they have sinned. It doesn't matter how rarely one sins, or what one's record is of how many days, weeks, months, or years one goes without doing a sin. A holy person may not know exactly how far they have come without doing particular sins, but they can see just how far they still must go. Even if they have freedom from doing certain sins, they will still experience concupiscence this side of Heaven, and they may "actually" give in to sin during weak moments.

Humility is very hard to see in others because we as humans can't see into the hearts of others and perceive their motives. We even have difficulty in seeing our own motives. Therefore, we need faith in Jesus the light. We need to trust Him that He will guide us, and lead the way into the beatific vision – the glory of God.

I also know that I haven't scratched the surface on what it means to practice humility. But I know this: Jesus is the final Word on humility. As the days, and weeks pass I am learning more and more about how to walk in the freedom to love that God promised me so many years ago. I am learning that I cannot focus on only one single principle to do this. The more we rush to and focus on one principle to the exclusion of other worthy truths, the more distorted our practice of love, humility, faith, and prayer will become. We need to be open to recalling when appropriate any of the truths that the Lord has revealed to us in the past up to the present. The Holy Spirit will reveal to us what we need at each moment to ensure a path to freedom and love! He will reveal new truths, and insights into older ones that we did not see before as is needed.

When one lives according to rigid rules of "right vs. wrong" or "good vs. evil" alone and measures oneself by them, then the focus is on the rules and oneself (not on God and people who we are called to love and can only do so, if we care for the people in ethical ways) and pride will be the natural outcome if one is successful. But when we abide in the true Vine – Jesus through faith and humility, then the focus won't be on us, and we won't attempt to conform to what humility looks like by our own efforts. Instead we will naturally love and find joy in Jesus because He is the true joy for those who discover His beauty. We will, if we patiently wait (search) for it, be transformed by God into clay lamps of His light and love.

God is self-sufficient and ultimately did not need us until He became man. He does not need us or our worship, but He desires it because it makes us healthy and He deserves it. God created us for LOVE: Himself. When we worship, we give ourselves in love to God. When we don't worship God, then we get proud and arrogant. And that pride leads away from authentic natural and supernatural loves and leads to envy, judging, greed, lust, sloth, gluttony, contempt, hatred, hurt, and death. I need to and want to worship God more and more because I still have lots of pride; besides loving God, and others as myself is really fulfilling. Jesus said the following:

> You say, 'I am rich; I have acquired wealth and do not need a thing.' But you do not realize that you are wretched, pitiful, poor, blind and naked. I counsel you to buy from me gold refined in the fire, so that you can become rich; and white clothes to wear, so that you can cover your shameful nakedness; and salve to put on your eyes, so that you can see. Those whom I love I rebuke and discipline. So be earnest, and repent.[95]

I had wondered for some time what the salve represented spiritually. I knew it was medicine that healed the eyes so that it could let light into them. So why do the eyes not let all the light in? Four words: pride or fear or guilt or lies. Pride, fear, guilt, and lies destroy our ability to see spiritually: either distorting or blocking it out completely. What is it in the salve that heals our pride or shame? God's touch: love is not that we first loved, but that God first loves us. Sometimes salve is the gentle touch (beauty, mercy, compassion, truth, or fullness of joy) from God that warms our hearts and helps us to see more clearly from our center. Otherwise it is the circumstances of life: illnesses, hardships, injuries, poverty, limitations, emptiness, pain, or suffering that come our way that purifies our gold: our hearts (together with the beliefs and desires that live there), so we become more capable of loving people and God as God desires. I have been touched in these ways.

---

[95] Revelation 3:17-19, (emphasis mine)

An approach that leads to humility is to not only seek to be a good person. Instead, seek to love out of caring for people in a way that does no harm to them. The former can be "I" focused. The latter is "other" focus. The former leads to pride and possibly seeking a reputation. The latter leads to healthy spiritual growth. It is wise to ask ourselves which one we are aiming for. The former can be more concerned with one's own honor, and invites conceit to play an unhealthy roll. The latter is concerned about others.

Many people see actions, or postures as evidence of humility. They will see carrying a Bible to church as evidence of their piety (but Hitler carried his Bible to church); they may see saying an eloquent prayer as being righteous but not realize they are proud and can be verbally abusive before or after the prayer; they might see saying forty-decades of the Rosary as a sign of piety but hold a grudge against the person who took their seat in the pew in the morning Mass last week.

Humility is managing our thoughts, emotions, attitudes, and relationships in a healthy manner. Holiness is about wholeness, and it is about spiritual health. It doesn't see its contribution to relationship with God or others as something to boast about. It is impressed with God, not one's own prayers, conduct, morals, values, or attributes.

I know that I am flawed in many ways. I still see my pride at work in my life every day even after much suffering. I have room to grow in becoming humbler. I know that, "there but for the grace of God go I." Lord God please show mercy to me a sinner. Thanks!!!

Some years ago I realized that we all need to give an account to God of ourselves when we die. At the time, I told myself that I did not fear this because I had tried so hard to overcome my sins with pain and failure being my wages for so much of it. I thought at the time that I had done my best and that God could not find fault with that. Problem is: God rewards faith not pride. God wants us to care. To care for others! Fact is I am making progress but only when God grants it. Yes, there have been a lot of failures. But also a lot of battles won through faith in Jesus. He gets the praise, the glory, and the booty.

Pride tries to control or manipulate things and people. Therefore, it looks for signs in one's circumstances for optimism or confidence that it's manipulating is going well. Only problem is circumstances change all the time, and people often don't give us what we want. Circumstances can have a lot of "cons" besides "pros". So, circumstances aren't a good place to find hope or security; so we feel insecure because we don't see the sure thing in our circumstances. To counter this, we need to look for hope in God not our circumstances. This requires faith and trust. Negative thoughts can enter the mind and make us feel down and insecure which re-enforce the negative thoughts that in turn re-enforces the negative feelings, etc. We got to renew our minds with correct thinking and right believing. Not all thoughts are to be trusted. Truth sets us free in our thoughts and our beliefs to grow in our love for people.

The first beatitude found in the Sermon on the Mount is:

"Blessed are the poor in spirit for theirs is the kingdom off heaven."[96] In today's language, this means, "Blessed are the humble for theirs is the kingdom of heaven." That is what the Sermon on the Mount hinges on. That is what this book hinges on. Not a false humility, but one that is nurtured through a relationship with God through Jesus Christ by faith. Faith is not a force that we muster and exert, or a technique that gets God's attention and makes Him love us more. No! "Faith is like opening a door that lets Jesus into our lives"[97], so we can talk with him and He with us, so that we can have community, and touch one another in love and grow in fellowship. This allows Him to grow us in love, and so be a blessing to other people we may know now and will still meet.

WHAT IS IMPORTANT?

It is that I remember the God who looks like Jesus: who came to undo the works of the devil. Who approaches us who are sinners yet with care, compassion, kindness, good intent, and peace. He is warmly affectionate, not rigid, not draconian, not coldly stern and not anally demanding. He smiles at me and draws me close. I am not an orphan spiritually. The maxims and principles above have their place but God is love and heals all things in His time.

Giving up pride is a day-to-day affair. But we can't get stuck only trying to put to death pride the rest of our lives, we got

---

[96] Matthew 5:3
[97] Summing up Derek Flood's thoughts in his unpublished book *Intimacy With God*, Cf. pp. 12-13, used with permission.

to grow humility too. Killing sin is half the battle; whereas seeking to love is the other half. Killing Pride's strongholds can be done. But there will always be battles. There is help[98] to kill pride and it's related strongholds and to replace them with humility and love.

When one sees progress in practicing the virtues of love, respect, humility, and kindness one should not hang one's hat on them and say: "See I'm good with God". Growth is good! Yay! But it is safer to see them as fruits from one's faith in Jesus. Faith saves us, not works, but faith without works is dead. Let's keep this tension in mind. It only takes one hole for a ship to sink. Thank God for the grace pump that keeps us from sinking because of our holes of sin, lack of understanding, blindness, and sour attitudes. God is a God of grace: unconditional love, patience, tolerance, compassion, reality, and peace.

---

[98] Cf. Rene Lafaut, *Dismantling the Tree of Knowledge of Good and Evil Within So Love Can Thrive*

23 CONCLUSION

I find it interesting how easy it was for me to expound on truths, ideals, humility, morality, love, and spiritual maxims when not exposed to raw reality where the stakes are high and life and choices and consequences did draw me to want to compromise.

A series I watched on TV made me more aware of this than ever. Under the right circumstance I bend, squirm, I get tempted, want to fold, want to give up (even if I don't give up), and I'm willing to compromise so I don't have to pay the price. Life is so tricky; sin is so sticky. I needed this film because it shows me that even though I have convictions, that when they get tested, doubts, fears, self-preservation, anger, weakness, temptation and the will to escape are not far from my will, longings, and thrust, or energy. So, I conclude that understanding humility is not the same as practicing it, or willing to pay the price to live it out, and to remain committed to it through thick and thin.

Another point that the Series raises, that I wrongly complained about in so many murder mysteries I watched on TV, in the cinemas, or read about in novels over the years, is that we often don't know who did it until the very end. And often the culprit isn't even a character in the story until very near the end. I am struck by how this scenario not only plays out in the murder mysteries all the time, but also in the situations in my life that have nothing to do with murder. I have found that I have assumed or jumped to the conclusion that I had all the evidence in front of me so many times only to realize later that I did not have the full picture. And would have made some pretty bad decisions if God had not convinced me to do so otherwise despite the pull on me to judge, passing sentence, and doing self-righteous things. Thank God for our consciences! We must all be vigilant and guard our hearts against counterfeit forms of honest pride (or humility) otherwise we will lose our dignity.

It is easier to see pride in other people than ourselves. We can do this religiously (even in church), not even knowing how to cure our pride in ourselves let alone any other person. We will always have some pride to battle against in this life. We know we have pride when we judge another person, no matter how right we feel in doing so. Jesus commands are not optional: judge not and condemn not!

Such is the battle. Of course, we can't completely overcome pride by ourselves, nor completely in this life. It isn't an all or nothing thing when it comes to how much pride and humility we have. Again, Jesus is the final Word on humility!

When God begins to make our footsteps firm, the temptation is to embrace ourselves as an authority on how things ought to be looked at, understood, and to think our opinions are absolute truth. One of the problems with this is that we become un teachable, proud, and then easily discount what others have to say and contribute. This is not a healthy way to live and causes us to disrespect people. Being convinced that we have absolute truth is very deceptive. We do not see all ends; only God does. I believe we can and do come to truthful conclusions, but truth always sets us free to love, be joyful, non-mechanical, warm, kind, humble, and to have neither lofty nor low opinions of oneself or others. A humble person is one who can let truth stand up for itself, and not seek honor when preaching it after having stumbled across it. Humility's aim is to love and build up, not tear down, marginalize, and put into boxes. Proud people not only put people into boxes but also truths, and land up forgetting and discounting both.

Again, we have humility when we grow in wholesome love. Put another way, there are three conditions for humility to be alive. They are:

1. Teachability. When we are not teachable we have pride.
2. Willing to get one's hands dirty. Getting our hands dirty means, we care enough to help bless other people.
3. Shown by how we treat others. When we respect people, cherish them, value them, and honor them, then we lose our sense of superiority, and we lose our conceit and arrogance.

Aiming for these alone will not necessarily bring them about. Correct theology is not enough to grow in love. Repentance is pivotal for love to grow warmer and more deeply in our hearts and relationships.[99]

---

[99] Cf. my book called, *Dismantling the Tree of Knowledge of Good and Evil Within So Love Can Thrive* for ideas on how to repent.

ABOUT THE AUTHOR

I lived my early life in South Africa, but have lived since then in Canada. I have struggled with Schizophrenia since 1992. I have struggled with many addictions. I am still fighting the fight of faith.
To contact me visit: www.brokenintofreedom.ca

BOOKS BY THE AUTHOR

Exploring Faith, Hope & Love
Dismantling the Tree of Knowledge of Good and Evil Within So Love Can Thrive
Contrasting Humility and Pride
Going Deeper With the Twelve Steps
To Be Broken into Freedom: A Spiritual Journey

If you like any of these books
please visit an Amazon website and leave a Review.

Printed in Great Britain
by Amazon

24905277R00099